Ian Addison

theguardian
teachernetwork
teachers.guardian.co.uk

Rising Stars UK Ltd, 7 Hatchers Mews, Bermondsey Street, London SE1 3GS

All facts are correct at time of going to press.

Published 2012
Text, design and layout © Rising Stars UK Ltd.

Editorial: Dawn Booth

Icon Design: David Thompson

Design: Words & Pictures Ltd, London

Cover Design: Mark Ecob

The publishers and author would like to thank the following for permission to use copyright images.

p.17 MyEBook, Colin Hill; p.18 both ZooBurst; p.20 both Wordle; Story map, Tom Barrett; p.23 MakeBeliefsComix.com; p.24 ICT Planning www. ictplanning.co.uk; p.36 Google Presentations; p.37 Prezi Inc.; Popplet, Notion Inc.; p.44 pencil.madness. com; p.45 Hockneyizer, BigHugeLabs; p.46 PopArt, BigHugeLabs; p.48 Paint.NET™, dotPDN LLC; p.48 Ian Tobin; p.55 Infant Encyclopedia, Simon Haughton; p.57 Zondle; p.59 Google Maps; p.63 Isle of Tune; p.64 Audacity; p.69 Pivot-Stick Man, SnapFiles; p.72 Movie-Maker®, Microsoft; p.75 ICT Planning www.ictplanning. co.uk; p.76 Games creation images, Tim Bleazard; p.78 Scratch, Lifelong Kindergarten Group, MIT Media Lab; p.78 Code, Tim Bleazard; Kodu®, Microsoft; p.83 Growing Plants, BBC; p.83 Rollercoaster Creator, © gamesgames.com; p.85 Coffee Shop Game, CoolMath; p.88 Sketch-Up; p.90 Google Maps; p.92 WordPress; p.93 Google Reader; p.95 Simon Haughton; p.98 St John the Baptist Primary School; p.100 Voki, Oddcast Inc.; p.103 PrimaryWall, Primary Technology ®, John McLear; p.103 QR code, Rising Stars UK Ltd; p.104 Delivr Corporation; p.107 Julian Wood; p.111 Poisson Rouge, ©Patric Turner; p.112 all Google Apps; p.114 Bit. ly; Microsoft Picture Manager; p.116 Animoto; p.116 bottom Google Maps; p.117 Animoto.

British Library Cataloguing-in-Publication Data.
A CIP record for this book is available from the British Library.
ISBN: 978-0-85769-586-4

Printed by Ashford Colour Press

About the author

Ian Addison is a primary school ICT coordinator from Hampshire who has been teaching since 2005. During that time he has been a leading ICT teacher and learning platform consultant for Hampshire. Since 2010 he has been a Google Apps for Education Certified Trainer and was also a co-creator of the Primary ICT group for Vital.

Ian has created a number of sites, including Under Ten Minutes (www.undertenminutes.com), to showcase a range of how-to videos for staff and children, and ICT Planning (www.ictplanning.co.uk) to share Primary ICT plans with other teachers.

Ian's blog – www.ianaddison.net

Ian's Twitter – @ianaddison

Acknowledgements

During the process of writing this book there have been many, many people who have helped with various elements. Some have helped to write a few pages, some have proofread sections, some have provided ideas for using tools in the classroom, some have shared links and ideas, and some have been there to help bounce ideas around with. They all have one thing in common though. I know them and have met them all through Twitter. More and more of what I learn is through these wonderful people who contribute their ideas online. I am lucky to have met many of them at conferences, events and meetings, and I would class many of them as friends too. Their constant enthusiasm, warmth and willingness to share are inspirational and I strive to do the same.

Twitter is mentioned in depth later in the book, but I have to say that it has totally changed the way in which I share ideas and collaborate with others. Having a network of like-minded teachers is essential. I know that if I have a lesson observation coming up, someone will share an idea. If I have a question, someone will answer it. If I have a bad day, someone will provide support, and if I have an amazing day, others will be there to help celebrate it.

It would be impossible to list everyone who has ever shared an idea with me, so I have listed those who have directly helped with the writing of this book. These include David Rogers for writing the section on Geocaching and Julian Wood for writing about QR codes.

I would also like to thank Tom Barrett for sharing his fantastic resources and giving me permission to include them in the book, to Mark Warner for creating so many great websites for teachers and for giving feedback on a draft copy of this book. Thanks also go to Miles Berry, Martin Burrett and Rob Smith for providing additional classroom ideas and links, and to Bev Evans and Ian Tobin for letting me use and adapt their help guides. An extra special thank you goes to Claire Lotriet for supporting me throughout this entire process, for providing additional ideas on a regular basis and for checking the writing as I went along. My thanks also go to the children of St John the Baptist Primary School for their amazing effort, enthusiasm and achievement with all areas of ICT.

If I could thank everyone who has ever supported me, inspired me, challenged me or shared with me, then I would. However I want them all to know that they are all very much valued and hugely appreciated.

Finally I would like to thank my parents for always supporting me and Charlotte, my partner, for her patience, her support, for letting me get on with my crazy plans and for not moaning when I work too much. I couldn't have done any of this without her.

About the contributors

Tom Barrett, Senior Consultant, NoTosh Ltd, gave permission to use www.edte.ch and Interesting Ways links.

Miles Berry, Senior Lecturer, Roehampton University, provided classroom ideas for using Scratch – www.milesberry.net

Martin Burrett, Primary School Teacher, Mersea Island School, Colchester. provided additional links and ideas – http://ictmagic.wikispaces.com

Claire Lotriet, Class Teacher and ICT Coordinator, Kensington Avenue Primary School, provided additional classroom ideas and proofread many sections – http://clairelotriet.com

David Rogers, Head of Geography, Priory School, Portsmouth, wrote the geocaching pages www.davidrogers.org.uk

Rob Smith, Key Stage 2 Teacher, Manchester provided ideas towards the 'video in the classroom' pages – http://great-teaching-ideas-weblinks.posterous.com/

Ian Tobin, ICT/Literacy Coordinator, Newhall Park Primary School, provided photographs for the green-screen image guide – http://newhallparkprimary.net

Mark Warner, ICT Coordinator, The Downs CE Primary School, gave permission to use his Ideas to Inspire links – www.teachingideas.co.uk

Julian Wood, Primary Assistand Headteacher, Sheffield, wrote the QR code pages – www.ideasfactory.me

CONTENTS

INTRODUCTION

Welcome to the *Essentials* guide to ICT. This book is aimed at teachers who wish to build their ICT confidence, explore new possibilities or simply learn something new. There is little argument that ICT is an integral part of children's lives now and will be even more pertinent in the future, so teachers need to find ways of using ICT within their classroom. This can be achieved in a number of ways, including class management and sharing learning or enhancing the opportunities provided for children.

The majority of ICT tools mentioned within this book are free, and there are many products that offer free versions with the chance to pay for more features if required. The tools mentioned can therefore be used quickly and easily within the classroom, many without lengthy teacher planning. The **internet** has changed in recent years and there are more and more web tools that allow users to not only view content that has been created, but also to create and publish their own. This is described by many as the second version of the internet – or **Web 2.0**.

Children enter school with more ICT knowledge than ever before, and have access to computers and other devices from a very young age. Teachers should be comfortable in sharing a variety of resources with children and try to go beyond what many consider as the norm. They must have the confidence to try new things where possible and keep up with developments in ICT. Although **hardware** is important (laptops, netbooks and mobile devices are certainly assets to any classroom), many of the ideas within this book can be used on any PC or mobile device (e.g. iPads, iPods, mobile phones, laptops) and, with a bit of consideration, will apply to almost any setting or classroom.

Structure

This book is divided into a number of chapters and is intended to be a resource that teachers can dip in and out of when the need arises. It begins with some tips to get the classroom ready for ICT, covering management of ICT as well as some basic hardware that should be made available. The chapters look at ways in which ICT can be integrated into existing subjects, such as literacy and numeracy, but also cover ICT-based topics such as animation, using audio and blogging.

Within each chapter a number of tools or ideas are introduced, explained and ideas provided for their use across the curriculum. There are also additional resources, such as **blog** posts, links to how-to guides and tips to get started. These tips may include notes about using the tool with a class or signing up to an account.

The end of the book provides guides to further **software**, useful ideas and how-to guides explaining ways to achieve some of the simpler tasks mentioned.

Key

Many ICT tools are referenced within this book – the key below outlines the categories into which they may fall.

 A tool that is available **online** using a **browser**. There may be **plugins** required (such as Flash or Java) but these tools should work in the majority of browsers.

 Users need to sign-in to access any of the features available.

 Users can create or use the tool without signing in, but if they wish to save or share their finished work, they will need a username. Or the website is open and there is no requirement for a username to use the service.

Sometimes a site will allow one username and **password** to be shared among a number of users, such as across the class. If this is the case then the username needs to be treated with respect and it would be sensible for the teacher to change the password after the lesson so children have restricted access at home. This will depend on the tool of course, but for shared accounts it helps to keep access to class use only.

 Relates to a piece of software that is installed on the computer, whether on one computer or across a network. Your school may have already installed this software on its system; if not then discuss this with the ICT coordinator and/or technician.

   The estimated time needed (2, 5 or 10 minutes) for someone to get started with and grasp the basics of a particular tool.

Useful links

Throughout the book there are links to a variety of websites and many of these have been shortened to make them easier to type into a browser. It is very important, especially for addresses that start with 'bit.ly', that these are typed into the address bar of the browser and not into a search engine. These addresses will not usually appear in the search results as they actually take the user somewhere else. One example of this is the shortened address http://bit.ly/STORYMAP which takes visitors to the (much longer) address http://maps.google.co.uk/maps/ms?ie=UTF8&hl=en&msa=0&msid=1067444699573 19968675.00048c463dcfd2cca9968&t=h&z=15.

There are a number of other links that refer to two sites: ICT Planning (www.ictplanning.co.uk) and Under Ten Minutes www.undertenminutes.com. The former has a selection of ICT plans and ideas to use within the primary classroom and the latter contains videos showing how to use various different software titles. To find resources on these sites, simply use the search boxes to find the content required.

Managing logins within school

As the use of online tools increases, so does the number of usernames and passwords that a child (or teacher) is expected to remember. There are ways of managing these and it is important to check whether the school has a policy for usernames.

It is useful to print a list of usernames for teachers to refer to and, for younger children especially, have a card for each student with his/her **login** details on and make this available to staff.

When using passwords it may be sensible to use a website such as www.howsecureismypassword.net to check password security. The simplest way to create a secure and memorable password is to choose two basic words the child can spell and put them together.

E-safety notes

Using online tools requires consideration of safety, for both the teacher and children. When using tools that enable discussion (e.g. email or social media), you should set sensible limits for the amount of time you spend on online communication with children, so it does not encrouch on the personal life of either children or yourself.

Using photographs

Before using photographs of children online it is good practice to ask parental permission. This works well when parents are given a form as part of the welcome pack when the child starts at the school, which should explain *how* and *why* photographs are going to be used by the school. A simple way of asking for permission is to list a few ways that they are likely to be used and then ask parents to tick yes or no boxes. It is useful to compile a list of which children are not allowed to have their photograph online.

Monitoring online content

Some online tools allow children not only to create content but also to view online galleries showing other people's work. Although this could be a great source of inspiration, they should always be checked in case there are inappropriate images or links to other unsuitable websites.

It is likely that children will come across inappropriate content as they work. Children need to know what to do if they see a website or receive a message that upsets them. Schools that have a procedure in place to monitor e-safety issues are in a much better position to deal with any problems that arise.

Many schools will have certain content blocked and unavailable for children. However, it is important to realise that they will usually have access to these sites at home. So teaching them how to use sites safely, and what to do if they feel threatened, you can help to prepare them for later life.

CHAPTER 1 GETTING YOUR CLASSROOM READY FOR ICT

Getting started

The basic equipment required for many of the projects within this book can be obtained fairly cheaply. In fact, your school may already have many of these resources. Look at this section as a list of tools that will help to create an ICT-ready classroom, or for use as a shopping list. There may be more than one of each of the following items in a classroom, but at least one of each is essential.

- digital camera (and a card reader)
- microphone
- batteries and a charger
- video camera
- visualiser
- interactive whiteboard.

Due to the nature of technology and the speed at which it changes, this book does not recommend which make or model to buy; it does, however, suggest some ideas to have in mind if you do need to go shopping.

Many schools have a shared collection of equipment, which can be stored appropriately in boxes, ready for use when needed. Within each box there could be a couple of cameras, a video camera and a selection of batteries and other tools. You will find that children take a great deal of care over this equipment and it is always useful to show them the strap that holds the camera and prevents it from being dropped.

It may be useful to nominate some of the children to be responsible for the box of equipment. It can be their job to look after the equipment, ensuring that is returned at the end of the day and that the batteries are charged, for example.

There are a number of devices, including the iPod Touch or BlackBerry Playbook, that will combine many of the functions of the items listed above, as well as providing a whole host of other tools. These definitely have a strong case for inclusion within the classroom but the primary focus of this chapter is the equipment that many schools either already have, such as PCs and laptops, or that can be purchased quite cheaply.

In addition, when it comes to implementing extra devices there needs to be much more of a strategic, whole-school approach to the rollout, whereas the equipment mentioned in this chapter can slot into any classroom with ease.

Digital camera

Digital cameras can be bought cheaply from supermarkets as well as **online**. There is a strong case for buying a larger number of cheap cameras rather than spending lots of money on a few, expensive models. When it comes to using images online, such as when blogging or adding them to the website, they will need to be in a lower resolution than the camera normally operates, in any case. Most cameras are around the 8–12 mega-**pixel** range but these produce large images which take up a lot of space on the camera, server and eventually your website. To change the resolution and size of images that have been taken, look at Chapter 13 for a simple guide. Changing the camera settings to around 3 or 5 **megapixels**, as shown in the photo, will make it quicker and easier to work with the finished photographs.

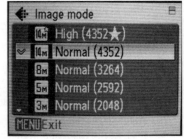

Camera settings

There is a range of memory cards available, although most now tend to come with **SD (secure digital) cards**. Whatever cameras are purchased by your school, try to ensure that the batteries and memory cards are the same brand to make it easier when replacing or adding to these items in the future. It makes sense to buy a memory card that is large enough for a range of photos but not so big that the teachers never need to clear the card! An 8 gigabyte (Gb) card should be ample.

Video camera

A pocket video camera is an essential tool for the classroom, to capture the children sharing their work, discussing a task or for use in a PE lesson. It can also be used to record part of a lesson, such as the introduction, which can then be replayed later for children who have struggled with a task. Some teachers have also recorded their introduction or the task and **uploaded** this onto their **blog** or virtual learning environment (**VLE**) so that the children can view it again while completing homework.

Not all videos have to be uploaded to the **internet** though; it is useful just to view back certain aspects of a lesson for evaluative purposes. This is particularly useful in PE so that the children can see themselves moving and then discuss what they were doing well and points for improvement.

As with digital cameras, there are different models and variants available. Key points include the quality of the video and how much the camera can hold. If possible, have a hands-on demonstration before purchase to see the quality of the recorded video. Many cameras have the ability to record in high definition (HD) too; this provides better quality video recordings but also means that the video files are larger and take up more storage space. You may find that the video camera takes still photographs or that the digital camera records video, so do check.

Microphone

There is a range of microphones that can be bought for use in school. There may also be a microphone already built-in to the laptop or computer and many **webcams** also have microphones built-in so do check this before purchasing more equipment. Generally, there are three different types of microphone:

- non-USB microphone (the top plug in the photograph)

- USB microphone (the bottom plug in the photograph)

- dictaphone style.

The non-**USB** microphone plugs directly into the computer – into the microphone socket – and has a connection similar to that on a pair of headphones, but with a different-colour connector.

USB microphones also plug directly into the computer and are more expensive than non-USB ones but produce a better quality of sound. Both these types of microphone will need to be connected to a computer in order to function. You will need **software** such as Audacity (http://audacity.sourceforge. net) or Sound Recorder (www.freesoundrecorder.net) to record the sound through the microphones onto the computer. Audacity will also convert the recorded file into an **MP3** should you need it.

The third type of microphone commonly found in classrooms is the TTS Easi-Speak microphone. These are dictaphone-style microphones in that they can be carried anywhere and do not need a computer to operate. This makes them ideal for taking on a school trip or out and about in the school grounds. To retrieve and edit the sound files, the microphone can be plugged into a USB slot on the computer. They also charge via USB.

Visualiser

This is the name given to a piece of equipment that looks like a webcam on a flexible neck. Their main purpose is to display things on a larger screen, such as the class whiteboard. This could be a child's piece of work, a diagram or part of a science investigation. It gives the teacher the ability to instantly share a piece of work, such as a story that a child has written, and then comment on it as a class. Using the whiteboard software, the writing can be annotated and assessed so that all the children can see it at once.

Some visualisers will have the ability to record videos or sound as well as still images. The image projected by the visualiser will be a live video, but having the ability to record what is seen can be very useful. This is particularly true in science where the visualiser could be used to demonstrate an experiment or investigation. This can then be replayed as required at a later date. For more ideas on how to use a visualiser in class, visit Ideas to Inspire (http://ideastoinspire.co.uk/).

Batteries and charger

This may be obvious, but giving each class its own set of rechargeable batteries and a charger will help to provide the children with a sense of ownership. It also means that they always have fully charged batteries to hand when required. This helps for those spontaneous moments when a camera is needed and removes the need to dash to a stock cupboard to check for batteries.

Interactive whiteboard and projectors

The majority of classes will have an interactive whiteboard installed and this will come with the whiteboard software to create flipcharts or presentations. The software tends to be ActivInspire, Smart Notebook or RM Easiteach, although others are also available.

There are different tools that can be used to enhance what is being shown on the screen. These include:

 Annotations: content on the screen can be annotated by the teacher or children. These annotations can be removed quickly or they can be saved for future reference.

 Backgrounds: use different backgrounds to enhance storytelling, e.g. a video that has been paused or a photograph. Put an image on the board and the children can stand in front of the board and act out their story.

 Lines and grids: use the different background templates to model handwriting. This can be recorded either using the built-in tools or a screen-recording tool, meaning that it is available to play back for future lessons if required. The grids and squared backgrounds can be used to model effective calculation strategies in maths.

 Reveal: can be used to hide a portion of the screen and then gradually share the content; this is useful when reading text from the screen. There are also spotlight tools that focus the attention on one particular portion of the screen.

 Sound recording tools: give children the opportunity to add their thoughts and responses to the flipchart.

Remember that the whiteboard can be used for so much more than just showing flipcharts and presentations. Think about using a tool such as Google Maps or Google Earth to explore the world on the large screen. **Skype** could be used to communicate with other classes or share webcams from around the world, such as safari cameras on www.africam.com.

When it comes to maintenance, it is important to ensure that the projector filter is cleaned regularly and that dust is removed. Make sure it is clear who is responsible for doing this.

Computer equipment and software

All the ideas throughout this book will work on any computer, but there are a few things to check before getting started. Most of the software requires the internet to work and as such there is a range of **plugins** that will need to be installed on the **browser**. These may already be in place and they may be managed by the **network** administrator.

> **Flash** – http://get.adobe.com/flashplayer/
> **Shockwave** – http://get.adobe.com/shockwave/
> **Silverlight®** – www.microsoft.com/getsilverlight
> For a more comprehensive list, visit the BBC WebWise site (www.bbc.co.uk/webwise/guides/what-plugins-do-i-need).

As for the browser, it is always sensible to keep up to date with the latest version of your internet browser, whether this is Internet Explorer (IE), Firefox, Chrome or Safari. Again these updates may be managed by the network administrator rather than the class teacher. Any recent browser should be able to manage all of the sites referred to in this book without any problems.

Generally, each class will have access to at least one computer or laptop that will be connected to the interactive whiteboard. There may be others throughout the school, such as those on a laptop trolley, but the class computer will be the most important part of the ICT-ready classroom.

With this in mind, it is important to ensure that it is looked after. In particular, if the class has a laptop, teachers should be careful when connecting and disconnecting the monitor/whiteboard lead as it is easily damaged.

With so many wires and connections around the computer it is important that health and safety issues are considered to ensure that children do not damage themselves or the equipment as they are moving around the room.

With all of these considerations in place, the classroom should now be prepared for ICT!

CHAPTER 2 DIGITAL PUBLISHING

Introduction

This chapter will showcase a range of different tools to aid the teaching of literacy in the classroom. There are a number of tools that can be used to help with various elements of the literacy curriculum. Many of these focus on storytelling but can also be used for non-fiction texts or poetry.

This chapter looks at:

 creating and publishing e-books   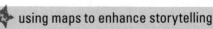 using maps to enhance storytelling

 using **online** tools to create stories   creating comic strips

 creating word **clouds**   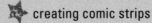 improving typing skills.

One benefit of using ICT is that almost any website will help to inspire a story or an idea. Imagine the wealth of pictures available online; how could these be used at the start of a literacy lesson? The children could imagine they are in that setting and describe what they can see, hear and smell. What about the endless, freely available video clips – could these be used to inspire writing? Children could write about what happens next, or think of an alternative ending. Or how about just listening to the soundtrack of an animation clip with no dialogue before watching it? Can children predict what is happening or what the film clip is about? Image and film can really hook the children when it comes to writing, and sourcing suitable examples has never been easier thanks to the **internet**.

With some ICT projects, such as green-screening (read about this on page 48), teachers have to think of new ways of planning and teaching, but with a comic strip or an e-book, they can just make small amendments to what they are doing already. ICT often gives you another mode of output so the children's final pieces of work make it beyond their exercise books. Through these first simple steps you can move on towards using a wide range of other tools with the children.

Almost any prompt can be used in some way to tell or share a story and the internet offers a range of tools to help make this easier. There is no need for any additional equipment for the tools in this section, other than a strong sense of imagination.

Publishing the written word: e-books

Getting started

Converting written words into an electronic format helps to give children a greater pride in their work as it can be shared with a larger audience more easily than if it remained in their literacy book or was glued to a wall. There are several websites (see below) that enable you to change images into an electronic book (e-book) or downloadable file that can then be added to a website, **blog** or **VLE**. They can also be shared via email as the sites will often provide a direct link to the e-book.

The websites work as follows:

1. Create a free account for the service.
2. Scan in the children's work to create images, use these images to help create pages.
3. Arrange your pages as required.
4. Include sounds, videos and other components if needed.
5. Produce the book for others to view.

These sites will often give you control over the privacy of the books that are produced. Users are then able to choose whether the books are completely public, private or a mixture of the two where visitors can only see the books if they have the direct link rather than searching for the book on the internet.

In the classroom

E-books are great for sharing and promoting learning and work from across the curriculum. This could include written work, stories, photographs and other aspects of the children's work over an entire topic. An e-book is the name given to a book that is created and viewed on an electronic device such as a computer. A key point is that this promotes the use of handwriting and not just typed text, meaning that children will not have to re-write their work to include it in the book.

Art

 As any work can be scanned, e-books make a fantastic way of sharing artwork online. For larger pieces, photographs may need to be taken. While children work, encourage them to scan their work and then use the e-book tool to add comments, discuss their choices and comment on the progress of their artwork.

Cross-curricular and whole school

 Create an e-book per child at the start of the year (junior-aged children should be able to manage these themselves). **Upload** excellent examples of work to the individual's e-book –

at the end of the year, the children will have an online portfolio of their learning for that year.

 Create a school prospectus. Your school may already have one in a **PDF** format, but uploading this to the e-book website and then putting a link on your school website adds an extra way for people to view it.

Design technology

 Create a how-to guide for making a model, giving instructions and showing the techniques used. Include a video of the model in action at the end of the book.

History

 When learning about a certain period in history, build up an information book documenting a subject that is interesting to the child, for example, the wives of King Henry VIII or the Tudor court. Include pictures and useful websites to enhance the book for the reader.

Literacy

 Create a poetry anthology or class storybook to share with younger children within the school, or create a dictionary of words learned throughout a particular topic.

 To aid teachers with writing moderation, collect pieces of writing at different levels that can be marked and assessed. Then create an e-book to share with teachers to provide a consistent approach to writing moderation.

Maths

 As a class or school, create a guide to maths strategies that may need to be learned, showing progression from addition in Year 1 through to addition in Year 6. This online resource could then be shared with children and parents as an aid to their future work.

PE

 Design and build up a portfolio of new games to play – share this with others to provide them with ideas for playtime.

Taking things further

Adding video and audio to e-books is slightly more complicated but adds a whole new level of enjoyment for the reader. Children could add narration to their written work to aid younger readers or add a video of them explaining how they drew the pictures that were included. This gives the books a more personal feel. Video can be used to help demonstrate a process – for example, in a book showcasing design technology work, it can show children working and creating a model and then the final model after it has been completed. Video can also be used as a way of sharing the children's evaluation at the end of the process.

Useful tips and resources

MyEBook – www.myebook.com Allows the user to create e-books online. Create an account, upload images, video, sound and more to create your books. To see some examples, look at www.myebook.com/mr_hill_3-4H.

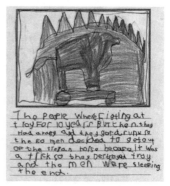

Part of a spread from MyEBook (courtesy Colin Hill).

Lulu – www.lulu.com Converts picture files, PDFs and Word documents into online books and will publish them onto Amazon and other online stores. Alternatively, on a much simpler level, the PDFs can be published on the school website.

Online storytelling

Getting started

These websites often have a 'light' version which is free and a premium version offering more features, such as the option to **download** the book to view **offline** or to add a greater number of pages in each book. Some also offer a way of managing a number of users (as well as creating usernames for the children) thus making them ideal to use in class, and enabling children to have their own online space in which to create books. ZooBurst (www.zooburst.com) also offers the option to see books from all the other children throughout the school, providing a great way of sharing examples of work.

These websites work as follows:

1. Create an account and sign-in.
2. Create a new book by adding images from the online gallery or uploading your own.
3. Add text to the pages and the characters.
4. Publish the book for others to see.

In the classroom

These tools provide a great way of writing storybooks for younger children, as they have colourful graphics and generally less room for text, meaning that shorter sentences can be used.

Storybird and ZooBurst provide users with a comprehensive collection of images and **clipart** that can be included within the book, but they enable users to upload their own images too. These can then be edited and manipulated within the story. Some of these tools will also allow users to add audio to the characters in the book, enabling another level of multimedia to be included.

Although these tools are designed for storytelling, they can be used in a variety of ways across the curriculum: enhance a presentation or present learning in a different way. Or maybe create a school prospectus with a difference, using uploaded photos of the school with children's commentary to give a different approach to the normal prospectus.

Uploading images in ZooBurst.

Taking things further

ZooBurst (see below) has an additional feature that includes Augmented Reality. Simply print the ZooBurst logo and hold it up to the **webcam**. This then projects the storybook onto the logo so that it appears to be on the table or coming out of the paper.

Useful tips and resources

Storybird – www.storybird.com Use the images in the gallery to help populate the story. There is also a paid-for element that allows users to purchase their online storybook as a paper copy.

ZooBurst – www.zooburst.com Creates a 'pop-up' book that can also be embedded into websites and blogs.

'Popped-up' images in ZooBurst.

Word clouds

Getting started

Word **clouds** are the names given to tools that take a selection of text, such as a news story, and display the text according to how popular/frequent certain words are. So the most popular words within the story will be larger than the others. Common words are usually omitted but there is usually on option to include them if you wish.

These websites work as follows:

1. Find a selection of text, or type into the box provided.

2. Change the font/style/colour.

3. PressGo/Done.

4. Print the image, save it to the computer or take a screenshot.

These tools are incredibly simple to use, yet provide an extremely effective way of displaying a piece of writing.

The main tools for creating word clouds are:

- **Tagxedo** – www.tagxedo.com (requires Silverlight®)
- **Wordle** – www.wordle.net (requires Java)
- **Word Clouds** – www.abcya.com/word_clouds.htm
- **Word It Out** – www.worditout.com

In the classroom

Art

 Describe a piece of art and display the words as a word cloud. How do children feel about the artwork? Type the words as the children call them out. Don't worry if there are duplicates, they will be enlarged on the word cloud.

Cross-curricular and whole school

 Children write about themselves, describing their likes and interests and paste them into Wordle.

 Find a news report from a website such as BBC News (www.bbc.co.uk/news) and see what the keywords are that appear in the cloud. Before creating the cloud, ask the children to predict the keywords that they would expect to see. For example, in 'Jack and the Beanstalk' the largest words should be 'Jack' and 'Giant'.

 Key Stage 1 classes often have a 'pupil of the day' or 'star of the week'. Ask other class members to suggest *why* the chosen child has been fantastic and collate these ideas into a word cloud to present to the child. To keep words together in Wordle, use the tilde (~) symbol.

 Use word clouds to evaluate reports, such as an Ofsted report. What are the keywords that emerge?

History

Use the words from a famous speech made by an important historical person such as Martin Luther King or Winston Churchill. What is his speech about? Does it still have impact when displayed differently? As a class discuss the keywords that appear within the cloud. Try showing the cloud before reading the speech. What is it about?

Literacy

Add text from books or poems into Wordle to discuss the key themes that come out.

Type 'said' three times (so that it appears larger each time) and then ask the children to suggest words to add. Once the cloud is created, print it and add it to a literacy display to aid future lessons.

Word Cloud for the word 'said'.

Print a Wordle with white writing, like the one shown on the right. Children could colour different words in different colours, for example all adjectives could be blue and adverbs red.

Word Cloud of a traditional tale. Which story is this?

Ask children to write a sentence to describe a word. Add these definitions into Wordle to create a class definition for the word.

Describe a character from a story. Collect the character traits and descriptions to create a class copy.

Enter the text from a book before reading it to the class, then ask the children to explain what they think the book might be about.

Maths

Collect different terms for maths vocabulary. For example, using 'multiplication' there could be: lots of, times, multiplied and product. Ask the children to collect words to add to the display.

Each child votes for his/her favourite colour, fruit or drink and displays the results in Wordle. This provides a different approach to data handling and could lead to discussions about the effectiveness of different approaches.

Useful tips and resources

Collecting a range of answers or feedback from children can take time, especially if all of them need to enter data into one box to create the word cloud. An efficient way of enabling all the children to add their ideas at once is a tool such as Primary Pad (www.primarypad.com). Another option is to create a simple Google Form that children can enter their data into and be copied into the word cloud later. A how-to video is available on Under Ten Minutes (www.undertenminutes.com).

One way of collecting words using a word cloud is to have the word cloud tool loaded on one computer and the children take turns to come and add their word to the box before you create the word cloud.

Some word cloud tools do not allow editing; to prevent any problems, copy and paste the text before pressing 'Go' so that if a spelling error is noticed the text will not need to be re-written.

Story maps

Getting started

As discussed in Chapter 6, Google Maps allows the user to add pins and markers to highlight key areas. These maps can also be collaborative so that children also add markers. Each marker can also have a description bubble to add additional information, as seen in the photo.

These maps can be used in many different ways, including storytelling. Tom Barrett shares this idea on his blog: http://edte.ch/blog/2010/08/01/google-maps-session-at-gtauk/. Tom started many resources and has shared them under a Creative Commons License (www.edte.ch/blog).

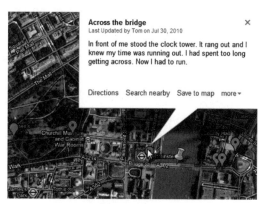

A story map (courtesy of Tom Barrett).

In the classroom

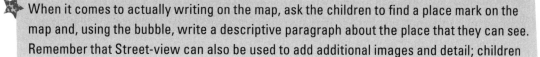

- Use imagery from Google Maps as a stimulus for writing. Castles and historical buildings, provide the children with a setting to describe. Using photos supplied by other users helps to provide different views, including night-time shots. Exploring different places around the world offers a huge wealth of photographs to stimulate writing.

- When it comes to actually writing on the map, ask the children to find a place mark on the map and, using the bubble, write a descriptive paragraph about the place that they can see. Remember that Street-view can also be used to add additional images and detail; children could use this to explore different settings for characters from their stories.

 Moving on, ask the children to create their own story map or pre-prepare one that they can begin to add place marks to in order to tell a story. Provide a beginning and ask children to use the line tool to draw a line to another place on the map. This could be the local park, a house that a character lives in or a train for their character to make a getaway. Once they have added the second landmark, they can use the description bubble to write a sentence or two in order to move the story along. Encourage children to use the additional tools available within Google Maps to enhance their writing, such as the photos provided by other users. Remember that descriptions can also contain images. The children could draw a picture of a character that they meet along the way and include this within their story.

Make use of the collaborative nature of Google Maps, and ask the children to write stories together. Provide a number of story maps that they can choose from.

Taking things further

For an example of story maps in action, visit Tom's map: http://bit.ly/STORYMAP.

These maps could also be used in a number of ways including charting the life of a historical character. For example, where was Florence Nightingale born? Where did she live? Where was the war that helped to make her name famous? Use place markers for these places to display a story of the character's life. Children could write diary entries for each marker from the point of view of the character.

Comic strips

Getting started

Some children will benefit from writing a story using pictures rather than text. This is when creating a comic strip is valuable. There are a few **apps** or downloadable tools, such as Comic Life (http://comiclife.com/) that will help to create comic strips, but MakeBeliefsComix (www.makebeliefscomix.com/) is a free website that will do a similar job.

The website works as follows:

1. Choose the characters and scenery from the online selection and add them to the first frame.
2. Move them around and resize as necessary.
3. Add speech/thought bubbles and text.
4. Print or email the finished comic strip.

Although these comic strips are not saved on the site, they can be downloaded as a picture file to keep for later. This also means that the comic strip could be put into a presentation tool, such as PowerPoint®, so that it could be built into a longer story than the normal three frames that are provided.

In the classroom

History

 Use the speech bubbles to discuss a key event in history, e.g. that Neil Armstrong has landed on the moon. Think about what the characters in the comic strip would say. Would they be shocked? Or excited? Do they believe it has happened?

Resizing a comic strip character. This comic was created at MakeBeliefsComix.com; go there to make your own.

Literacy

Have a character explaining a word type, e.g. an adverb, to another, including examples in the speech bubbles. Think about what an adverb is and how to explain it to someone else.

Build up a story over a number of comic strips. Write one comic strip a day to tell the story over the course of a week. Save the comic strips to develop into a continual comic book.

Maths

Describe how to solve a problem using just three frames of the comic strip. Think about how to partition numbers to add them together. Encouraging the children to explain the steps needed to approach the problem will help to consolidate their learning of the method. The comic strip could be printed in a larger size to use on the wall as a revision tool.

Make a comic strip where two characters discuss and define mathematical vocabulary, explaining the differences and similarities between words such as 'product' and 'multiply'.

Modern foreign languages

Write a conversation between two people in another language. Think about a simple conversation where one character asks the other for his/her name, age or place of birth. Building up conversations, rather than just learning the questions in isolation, will help to enhance children's learning of the language.

Science

⭐ Explain how a particular scientific concept works, such as evaporation. Children could set out the steps required in the evaporation process and use these comic strips as a reminder in the future.

⭐ Think about how to explain the notion of fair testing. The children use the characters to discuss the variables for a test they are conducting.

Useful tips and resources

There is an education section on both MakeBeliefsComix (www.makebeliefscomix.com/) and Comic Life (www.plasq.com) which lists some ways of using comic strips in the classroom. These will obviously apply to other comic strip tools too. To find more comic strip tools, visit http://bit.ly/comicstrips.

Typing skills

Getting started

Although learning how to type does not sound like an exciting task, it is an activity that should be included within the primary curriculum. There are a number of tools that will help children to improve their speed and efficiency when typing and these activities work well as a quick starter before an ICT lesson. While a child waits for other children to logon to their computers, he/she can use the time to load a quick typing game. It is therefore useful if these kinds of activity are linked on the school website or blog so that the children are able to find them quickly; they may also wish to use them at home. Children who practise these activities will soon become quicker at typing and this will help to reduce frustration when they are entering text into a range of different tools.

Useful tips and resources

Links are available on the ICT Planning website (www.ictplanning.co.uk) to various typing games including: Tidepool; Keyman; Typing of the Ghosts, Super Hyper Spider Typer; and many others.

Super Hyper Spider Typer

CHAPTER 3 ICT AND MATHS

Introduction

There are hundreds of tools and websites available to assist with teaching maths. Some of them offer activities and games for children to play independently in order to help improve their mental maths skills; others provide teaching tools to share an idea with the class.

This chapter covers:

- sites that provide maths games to challenge children
- data-handling tools
- games to help with times tables
- sites to help with a range of maths opportunities
- using maps to help teach maths.

It is helpful for children if websites are linked on the school website or **blog** as it enables easier access at home. When creating a list of links, make it a collaborative task: it is worth asking your children if they use any **online** maths games that they would recommend to their friends. You may be surprised at how clued-up they are. There are many areas of maths, such as times tables, where repetition is useful to help secure knowledge. As many online maths resources are presented as games, children often feel motivated to revisit these games and improve upon their time and score.

Try not to associate maths and ICT with mental maths games only. There is a huge amount of how-to videos online, which can put a new spin on maths teaching. Why not think about **embedding** one of these videos into your blog before teaching the topic in your maths lesson? This gives children a chance to become familiar with a topic or skill beforehand; they can then come to the lesson already having had some teaching input and armed with questions about what they didn't understand, or are possibly ready to tackle a problem straight away. Your gifted and talented mathematicians could even make their own how-to maths videos for the rest of the class or for younger children in the school. This could be done using screen-casting **software** or simply a video camera pointed at someone using a personal whiteboard or piece of paper and a pencil.

If you conduct a weekly mental maths or times-table test, consider recording the scores on a spreadsheet that you update and share with the children. If their score improves, it could be coloured in green. I have seen children motivated to improve their score so they can 'go green'. You could also turn these results into something more visual like a graph so the children can actually see their progress.

Maths websites

Getting started

Some sites provide children with a secure area in which they can play maths games on a range of topics. These sites require **logins** for access and the children's scores are recorded. Some offer the chance to challenge other children in the class, the school or even around the world, adding a competitive element to the games.

This is how these websites work:

1. Children login to the site using their details.
2. They either access the games that have been assigned to them or choose from an available range.
3. Scores are recorded for the teacher to look at later.

The main free sites for these maths games are Sumdog (www.sumdog.com), Tutpup (www.tutpup.com) and Managhigh (www.mangahigh.com). They all work slightly differently but follow a similar idea. They can also be used on the whiteboard with the class. The high-speed nature of these games helps to increase the children's ability to solve problems mentally.

Sumdog

Once registered for Sumdog (www.sumdog.com) users are provided with a range of games to play. The scores for these games are recorded and stored for each user. Children can be grouped together in the school so that they can play against each other. As games are played, the children earn coins and move up the ladder. These coins can also be used in the shop to help re-design their **avatar**.

Tutpup

The usernames on this site, e.g. brownfish3224, are not related to children's names. The activities on Tutpup (www.tutpup.com) include times-table games as well as sums using the four operators. When playing a game, the children are up against another user elsewhere on the system; this adds a competitive element and challenges children to try and reach a higher position on the leader board.

Mangahigh

Mangahigh (www.mangahigh.com) is much more advanced than the other two and is freely available to UK schools. There are over 400 games covering all areas of the maths curriculum from Key Stage 2 upwards. This helps to challenge the more able children, as the games continue through to secondary level. Scores are recorded on the leader board for each activity. One way of challenging children is to create a pupil account for the teacher and then play the game. This will give them a target score to try and aim towards (providing you score more highly than they do of course!).

You also have the option to assign games to the children so that they play games at an appropriate level rather than being given free choice to pick any activity on the site.

Mangahigh also has a feature known as a 'Fai-to' where one school is pitted against another. The school that scores the most points in a short period is crowned the winner.

Maths ideas

Getting started

A range of tools are available to help with teaching maths in the classroom. Some of these will be useful for the children to explore independently, others will be valuable as a teaching tool for use on the whiteboard. A great place to start is the ICTmagic site (http://ictmagic.wikispaces.com/Maths) as this has numerous resources for all areas of maths and is constantly being updated.

Times tables

Practising times tables is essential and some children will benefit from playing games designed to help them acquire this knowledge. There are many sites offering games to help support times tables, such as Grand Prix (http://bit.ly/timesgrandprix) and Penguin Jump (http://bit.ly/penguinsjump). One way of helping children is to provide a page such as http://bit.ly/stjohnshome, which provides links to times-tables games for the children to use at home. These games also work well on the whiteboard.

More times-tables games can be found on the Woodlands Junior site (http://bit.ly/woodlandstimes).

Data handling

Demonstrating the creation of graphs to children is an important task, providing they are given the chance to create one too. If the purpose of the lesson is data analysis, then you will be looking for quick ways in which to create a graph for the children to interpret.

Drawing a pie chart on a whiteboard can be a tricky task but, providing the percentages have been worked out already, Pie Color (http://piecolor.com/) will generate in seconds. Another tool is NCES (http://1.usa.gov/graphchart) which can also be used to create bar charts and other forms of graph.

There are a couple of pictogram creators online: a relatively basic one from Numbers Index (http://bit.ly/pictogram) and a more sophisticated tool on the Primary Technology Pictograph creator (http://primaryschoolict.com/pictograph/), which does not include any images to begin with. This works with the user labelling the axis and the tool searching for a picture that relates to the words.

For younger children who may be sorting data into groups, try Furbles (http://bit.ly/furbles), an activity with creatures called Furbles that need to be sorted into groups, e.g. based on their colour, number of eyes or their shape. These groups can also be represented by a graph or pie chart.

van

Decimals, fractions and percentages

When teaching fractions, a good place to start is Fraction Golf (http://bit.ly/fractiongolf) – this asks children to set the power bar to match a certain fraction; if correct then the ball goes into the hole. To find simple equivalent fractions, Flashy Maths (www.flashymaths.co.uk/swf/matcher.swf) is useful. This type of game could easily be made using 2DIY, so use this as an example and then ask the children to create their own. They could also mix decimals and percentages in the same game.

Search results for 'van' in Pictograph.

The BBC offers a game (http://bbc.in/bbcdecimals) that teaches decimals. Follow the story and work out the different problems involving decimals.

Patterns

When teaching patterns, it would be useful to start with this tool from ABCya (www.abcya.com/patterns.htm), which looks at the sequence of colours to find a pattern. You could then move on to Blob Kid (http://bit.ly/blobkid), which challenges children to find the missing numbers using a 100 square. The numbers can be changed to take the game from a simple exercise to one that requires more thought. The Line Dry game (http://bit.ly/numberdry) shows a number sequence with a missing number, and the children then fill in the missing box. For more of a challenge, Battleship Numberline (http://bit.ly/numberships) provides a couple of numbers on a number line – children then find the missing numbers and are given scores for accuracy.

Time

There are many great games for teaching time, including Bang on Time (http://bit.ly/stoptheclocktime) and Doorway About Time (http://bit.ly/doorwaytime). The benefit of using these resources is that the clock can be made large enough for the children to see it. These activities work well if the children join in together, perhaps using their own small clocks to match the time shown on the board. Clock Spin (http://bit.ly/clockspin) is a particularly useful online clock as the minute hand and hour hand move together, making it easier to demonstrate the effect of time passing.

More ideas

Countdown – http://bit.ly/subcountdown Useful for a quick starter activity. It plays in a similar way to the TV programme *Countdown*. Choose a selection of numbers and try to reach the target. There is a timer but for less able children this does not need to be used. It may also be worth offering points for children who get the closest, as some targets are very challenging! The site also has a letters game which is useful in other lessons.

iboard – www.iboard.co.uk Contains a huge array of games and teaching activities. Although initially aimed at Key Stage 1, the site has now developed to cover Key Stage 2 as well. There are some great activities for teaching money, counting and time as well as resources such as online arrow cards to help with the teaching of place value. The majority of the activities are free but for a small annual fee there is the chance to access further resources.

Jig Saw Doku – http://bit.ly/jigsawdoku A simple Sodoku game for children. There is also a timer to provide an element of challenge.

Primary Games Arena – www.primarygamesarena.com A primary site hosting a variety of games that cover all subjects, with useful links to maths games.

Splat Square – http://bit.ly/splat100 This is a simple 100 square that can be used to count on or back in different numbers.

What's My Angle? – http://bit.ly/whatsmyangle A simple site that shows an angle and an online protractor – very useful for demonstrating how to use a protractor to find a range of angles of differing sizes.

Maths Maps

Tom Barrett's Maths Maps (http://edte.ch/blog/maths-maps/) are a great way of encouraging children to explore a range of maths ideas and concepts based around their local area, or anywhere in the world. The site has maps to use but it does not take too much effort to make one of your own.

The maps on the site have a range of pins attached, each with a maths question; some are simple and can be answered immediately, others require a bit of exploring on the map. For example, one of the Nottingham data-handling questions asks the children to zoom in to look at the road signs around the roundabout and create a graph to show how often each letter appears. Although this sort of task could easily be replicated using any piece of text, the map helps to engage the children and gives a different approach to the task.

Creating a map for your class is simple, and children could help write the questions. Chapter 6 addresses how to create maps and related videos can be found on the website Under Ten Minutes (www.undertenminutes.com).

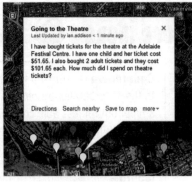

Example of a Maths Map question (courtesy of Tom Barrett).

The key elements to creating a Maths Map include:

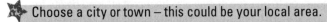 Choose a city or town – this could be your local area.

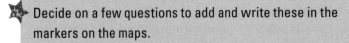 Explore the look of the town, zoom in closer to see detail and also use Street View.

Decide on a few questions to add and write these in the markers on the maps.

Share the map with others – this could also include sharing it with Tom on his site.

It is also useful to think about the colour of the pins too. The colours could either relate to ability or to the area of maths; for example, red markers relate to shape questions but green indicate data handling.

Remember that maps can be collaborative, so sharing them encourages others to contribute. This will help to add a range of questions to the map and build it into an even more useful resource.

CHAPTER 4 PRESENTATIONS

Introduction

With greater frequency we expect children to present their learning to others: at the end of a topic, as part of their homework or just as an element of the lesson. It is therefore important that children are given the opportunity to practise presentation skills.

A number of different tools help children to present information to an audience, ranging from the traditional, such as PowerPoint®, to collaborative presentations that will enable children to work together on a shared presentation.

Presenting to an audience begins when children are very young and they share their work with a friend. It is important that they have a chance to articulate what their picture is of and how they made it. Children are also given the chance to talk to an audience as part of show-and-tell style sessions. This can help to build their confidence when presenting at a later date.

A good presenter has good speaking and listening skills and engages the audience, using his/her slides as a tool to help get the message across.

This chapter covers the key elements of a good presentation, which include:

 Facing the audience – possibly at an angle so that the presenter can see the board too.

 Having brief notes or being able to talk without reading the text directly from the screen.

 Using **software** to create key messages and support the verbal aspect of the presentation.

 Not using flashy tricks or effects which detract from the purpose of the presentation.

PowerPoint® is one of many tools that are used to present information to an audience. It also provides a good opportunity for you to think about the key elements of the presentation rather than the transitions or animation effects. Knowing how to use these effects is one thing; knowing when to use them is another. The purpose of this chapter is to share some tips for using PowerPoint®, as well as exploring some of the better-known presentation tools that are available **online**.

In the classroom

Although the core element of these presentation tools is to present information, they can be used in a number of different ways. Rather than being projected in front of an audience, they can also be driven by a user on one computer. This works well if there is a process that needs to be broken into a number of stages, with each stage being shared on a different slide. The inclusion of hyperlinks enables the user to navigate through the slides in a non-linear fashion, and a contents page helps to guide the readers, who can then click to see the different aspects of the presentation and choose their own journey through all the information.

Art

 Talk the viewer through the journey of a piece of art. Art lessons often start with an example piece from an artist, so show this as the first slide and then pictures of plans, trials and experimentations leading up to the final piece of the child's artwork.

Design technology

 Use each slide as a basis for the plan when creating a model. Take photos to document the process and create a how-to guide for others to follow. Start by taking pictures of the materials used in the model and then include photographs and notes throughout, building up to the final model on the last slide.

Literacy

 Use the slides to build up a sentence. Write a simple sentence on the first slide, copy this to the second but add an adjective. On the third slide add an adverb and so on.

 Represent part of a story on each slide, either using a picture and a few lines or a paragraph of text.

 Compile a sentence or word bank, with each slide having a type of word, maybe a connective or a simile. Children then add their own ideas to build this into a class resource.

 Create a class dictionary for the current topic/theme. On each page present a new word that has been learned, along with a description and definition, and any images or related links.

 Title each slide with a story genre and then collect examples of books that fall into that genre to create a class reading list. Ask the children to review the books that they have read and add these reviews, written or spoken, to the slides.

 Use each slide as a diary entry for either a real diary or that of a traditional character. Think about what the character would say each day and what might have happened to him/her.

 Create a 'class emotions' thesaurus. Designate a different word to each slide, e.g. 'happy', 'angry' and 'tired' – take photos of the children acting out that emotion and insert into the slide. Arrange alternative words that mean the same thing around it. Include images to enhance the words, videos of children acting out scenarios that might make them, for example, angry, and include ways to change this emotion.

Maths

 Use the slides to show a step-by-step guide to solving a problem – start with the task at hand and use each slide to break it down into steps for others to follow. Teachers could also create these step-by-step guides for complex tasks such as simplifying fractions or working out the grid method for multiplication.

 Create a multiple-choice maths quiz. Each child contributes a question and sets it on his/her slide. Three choices of answer are given with the wrong ones linked to an 'incorrect' slide and the right one linked to a 'you're correct' slide.

PSHE

 Create a presentation about someone else in the class as a 'getting to know you' exercise at the beginning of term. Provide a set of headings, e.g. favourite things, first memory, etc., or ask the children to think of their own.

Science

 Use a different slide for each stage (prediction, results, conclusion, etc.) of a science investigation. Include notes and photos to document the steps and/or links to videos about the subject. As the investigation progresses, add notes to the slides explaining the process.

Whole school

 Ask the children to create a school tour or prospectus for others to look through when visiting the school. Each slide could show a different area of the school with a title or contents page that links them all together.

PowerPoint®

Getting started

PowerPoint® is installed on many school and home computers, and is therefore often the first port of call when designing a presentation.

This is how PowerPoint® works:

1. Slides are created, with each slide containing text, images, links or videos.
2. Colours and layouts can be edited.
3. Animations may be added to make the text appear at different intervals.

Using the Design tab, users can change the layout and colour schemes of the slides. There is also the option to change the font style and this will affect the whole look of the presentation.

Users can also add effects when the slides change, and these are known as Transitions. These changes can either be timed or they can happen automatically after the previous effect – they do not necessarily rely on a mouse-click.

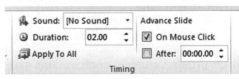

The timing **menu**

Within the Slideshow tab is the option to have the presentation continue without a user present. This is useful while visitors are looking around the school or at a parents' evening as a way of presenting photos or information.

Taking things further

Within PowerPoint® is the option to include hyperlinks that not only link users to websites but also to pages within the document (the table on the following page shows how this is done). This means that, with the inclusion of a contents page, children can produce a non-linear presentation.

To do this, create the presentation as normal with each slide covering a different aspect of the subject matter. Once the slides have been created, make a contents page that lists the different sub-sections throughout the slideshow, by creating hyperlinks as shown on the next page.

Non-linear presentations work very well for non-fiction content as they reinforce that the text can be read in any order. This supports the non-chronological texts written in literacy lessons. This style of presentation is also possible for a 'choose your own ending' story. As the viewers reach a certain point in the story, they can click on option A or option B.

Useful tips and resources

To see more examples of how PowerPoint® has been used for numerous purposes, including storytelling, take a look at Simon Haughton's **blog**: www.simonhaughton.co.uk/powerpoint/.

The following table shows how to create a hyperlink.

To create a hyperlink, highlight the word on the contents page and right-click. Choose Hyperlink.	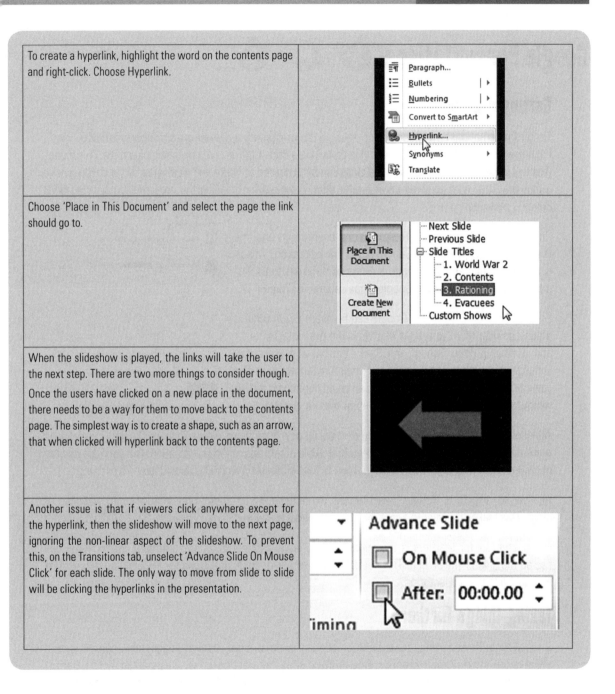
Choose 'Place in This Document' and select the page the link should go to.	
When the slideshow is played, the links will take the user to the next step. There are two more things to consider though. Once the users have clicked on a new place in the document, there needs to be a way for them to move back to the contents page. The simplest way is to create a shape, such as an arrow, that when clicked will hyperlink back to the contents page.	
Another issue is that if viewers click anywhere except for the hyperlink, then the slideshow will move to the next page, ignoring the non-linear aspect of the slideshow. To prevent this, on the Transitions tab, unselect 'Advance Slide On Mouse Click' for each slide. The only way to move from slide to slide will be clicking the hyperlinks in the presentation.	

Google Presentations

Getting started

Google Presentations (www.google.com/google-d-s-presentations/) work in a similar way to PowerPoint®, but there are some differences. The first is that Google Presentations are only available online. This means that any presentation started during a class can be accessed at home and vice versa. So, if children have a task that they wish to continue at a later date, the need for emailing the presentation or using **USB** drives is removed.

The sharing screen

Children need a **login** to create their own presentations and this is usually managed through Google **Apps** for Education. This is a suite of resources that provide a range of different tools. For more information, check the Google Apps section in Chapter 12.

Presentations created within Google can be shared with others, either allowing them to access and view the presentation or to edit it. This is done through the Share button, and users can choose which other people can edit their presentation at the same time. These people then receive an email containing a **URL** which takes them to an editable version of the presentation.

Although this sounds chaotic, and often is, it opens up a huge range of possibilities. Children can work on presentations in groups, with some researching while others add to the presentation. The optimum number of children per group is probably around three or four, although Google Docs could have 25 or more.

Another key aspect of Google Presentations is the capacity to embed presentations into websites or blogs. This makes it easier to share the content with a wider audience.

One useful tool for teachers is the opportunity to leave comments on presentations that children can see on the side of the screen. This could be spelling corrections, questions for the child or suggestions for improving the presentation.

Taking things further

Some Google Presentations have been embedded in other sites, so that suggestions can be shared about improving classroom practice. One of these sites, 'Interesting ways', was started by Tom Barrett and is listed on his blog (www.edte.ch/blog) and others have been compiled on Mark Warner's site (www.ideastoinspire.co.uk). These ideas have quickly developed into a range of presentations on a number of topics.

Prezi

Getting started

Prezi (http://prezi.com) is a presentation and mind-map tool. It offers a blank screen on which to add text and images. Content can be placed on the screen in any order and in any position, with the option of deciding the final presentation order later.

This is how Prezi works:

1. Sign up to a free account.
2. Create a Prezi presentation by double-clicking anywhere.
3. Choose a background or design layout.
4. Link ideas together using frames and lines.
5. Decide on the running order for the presentation.
6. Share it or embed into a blog or website.

Try and group ideas and content together in similar areas of the screen. When deciding the order in which text and images will be presented, having them organised as such makes it easier to display them.

Taking things further

An education version of Prezi allows children and teachers more storage space than regular users. To sign up to this, you need to use the school or college email address.

Presentations created in Prezi can be **downloaded** to run on computers without an **internet** connection.

Upload your PowerPoint® document and Prezi will convert the file into the Prezi format.

Through a shared URL, users can work on the same document to create a presentation together. This works particularly well in the classroom as a way of brainstorming ideas among a group of children.

TOP TIP

When using Prezi, be aware that the spinning nature of the content can be a little disorientating for some audiences.

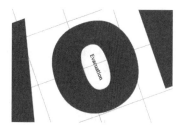

Small text included within larger text.

The path tool links ideas together.

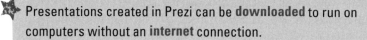

Popplet

Getting started

Popplet (http://popplet.com) works in a similar way to Prezi in that it provides a blank space to which users can add. Each new addition, or Popple, is put into a box (in contrast to the more free-form nature of Prezi). These Popples can be moved around and linked together, making it simple to join ideas to give them structure.

This is how Popplet works:

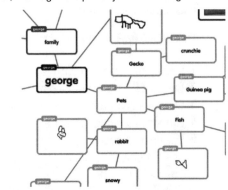
Popples linked together.

1. Sign up to a free account.
2. Create a box or Popple by double-clicking anywhere.
3. Choose a background colour.
4. Link ideas together using lines and arrows.
5. Add additional content such as **weblinks**, Flickr pictures or videos.

Taking things further

Popplet presentations can be downloaded to run on computers without an **internet** connection. They can also be saved as picture files which could be compiled into a slideshow to showcase children's presentations. As with Prezi, a collaborative feature within Popplet allows different users to work on the same presentation simultaneously.

In the classroom

Prezi and Popplet can be used in similar ways within the classroom, and the ideas below will work with either website. They can be used to organise as well as present ideas, and are useful for planning a project, story or task.

History

 Create a timeline to showcase the area of history currently being studied. Add key dates/ events and information as work on the topic progresses.

Geography

 Compare and contrast two different settings or countries. Use headings such as currency and link countries to these. Popplet also allows Google Maps to be added.

Literacy

 Plan a story. Plot the main headings, e.g. character, setting, problem, solution – ask the children to add additional information relating to each heading.

Maths

 Collect vocabulary, e.g. different words for 'multiply', or a range of 2D shapes, and present them as a mind-map.

 Create a collaborative Popplet with a number in the middle. Each Popple coming away from the centre shows a different way of making this target number. For example, for a target number of 24, 'Popples' could include 6×4, 2×12 or $20 + 4$.

Science

 Plan a science investigation with each frame or area representing a different stage, e.g. planning, method and conclusion. Add results to each area using pictures or video.

Useful tips and resources

How-to guides for both Prezi and Popplet are available on Under Ten Minutes (www.undertenminutes. com).

Whiteboard software

Whiteboard software is often overlooked as a presentation tool within the classroom. Although teachers use this regularly, children rarely have access to it when creating presentations.

Popular whiteboard software found in schools includes ActivInspire, Smart or RM Easiteach. For creating presentations, it can be an ideal tool for children.

Whiteboard software can offer the following features:

 A range of pages (slides) to contain information, hyperlinks and images.

 The option to select from a pre-existing library of content ranging from shapes and symbols to **clipart**-style images.

 The option to import images from other sources.

 A voice-recording tool which gives the flipchart an audio.

CHAPTER 5 DIGITAL IMAGERY

Introduction

Images can be used to stimulate discussion, promote enquiry or share an experience with an audience. Cameras are already plentiful within schools and the majority of people are happy to take and use photos of learning as evidence. But what happens to those pictures once they have been taken? How can they be used in different ways?

This chapter looks at how teachers and children can create interesting images or breathe new life into existing pictures. It also investigates how pictures can be edited to create entirely new images that may be used across the curriculum in a variety of ways: to aid learning, showcase children's achievements or enhance an aspect of a particular topic. Adding images to a website or **blog** as a way of sharing them with a wider audience is a further aspect included here.

This chapter covers:

- creating video slideshows for use **online**
- using a range of online art tools to edit and enhance images
- tools that edit or enhance images in less than one minute
- creating Hollywood-style effects using green-screen
- viewing artistic masterpieces from your chair
- a range of tools to change your photo into an artistic masterpiece.

As this chapter discusses the use of digital images (some of which will be of children), it is advisable to read 'Using photographs' on page 8.

It is also worth considering how often children are given the chance to take photographs in class. Where appropriate, the children should be given the opportunity to use a camera from a young age; after all, many will be used to doing so at home. As they get older, perhaps around Year 3, show them how to transfer images from the camera to the computer.

Photo slideshows

Getting started

Photo slideshows enhance the learning experience by adding dynamic and engaging elements. Many websites allow you to **upload** photos easily and show these as a video slideshow, with text and audio accompaniment if desired. The majority of sites require the user to register (using an email address) and, although some charge a fee or subscription, many feature a 'lite' version that is free. Animoto (www. animoto.com) and PhotoPeach (www.photopeach.com) are examples of websites that facilitate the creation of dynamic, video-based slideshows that enable children to tell stories, illustrate processes and enliven their presentations. Animoto provides a free 30-second video for all users and the full subscription service offers longer videos. Some websites also supply education licenses making class use simpler, and a shared account for the school can make it easier to keep videos in one place.

This is how these websites work:

1. **Login** and select a theme or template.
2. Select a range of photos to include within the slideshow.
3. Follow instructions to upload photos – often multiple files can be uploaded at once (hold CTRL on a PC or CMD on a MAC to select more than one file at a time).
4. Rearrange or remove photos if necessary.
5. Add text to provide additional information or create a narrative for the slideshow. Sometimes audio files can also be added (usually as **MP3** files) to create a background audio track or dialogue.
6. Wait briefly while the site creates or mixes the slideshow together.

Once children have created their slideshows, they are able to share their work with others. Sites provide 'embed codes' and links which can be used for sharing the work on blogs, or other social media **networks.** There is also an option for children to edit and remix the video to improve their work. Some sites will allow the videos to be **downloaded** so that they can be viewed **offline**, although there may be a charge for this feature. These sites usually have a wide selection of music and audio tracks that can be included within the video. They also sometimes include searches on other sites, such as YouTube (www.youtube.com), but the library on the site is often sufficient for most users.

In the classroom

If you have photographs, then you can create a slideshow, which have a multitude of uses within the classroom or school context.

Art

 Produce an 'online gallery' of children's artworks, e.g. to display at a parents' evening. Intersperse this with examples that inspired the children's pictures. Include 'work-in-progress' shots to show how the final piece was created.

Cross-curricular and whole school

 Ask children to use Animoto to create a 'school tour' to post on the school website.

 Use photo slideshows to share experiences from residential visits, school trips or theatre productions, both with other children within the school and with parents.

Design technology

 Present the stages of a project, from the 'raw materials' at the start, to the finished item. This would work equally well for making a model and as a way of documenting the process. Include videos within the final slideshow.

Literacy

 Ask children to illustrate their stories with pictures they have drawn or photographs they have taken. Use the slideshow to demonstrate the range of illustrations for the characters within the story.

 Write stories for younger users. As Animoto allows a sentence to be included between each picture, use this as the text of the story, explaining, as the pictures scroll through, what happens to the characters.

 Provide the children with a picture of a character from a story, around which they should describe his/her appearance and personality.

Maths

 Present the stages of a calculation, e.g. how to solve a multiplication problem, as a sequence – include photographs or video of the 'working out', interspersed with text and audio to explain each stage. This could be used for peer-tutoring and reinforcing understanding.

 Create a slideshow with a range of 2D and 3D shapes. Use the text feature to label the shapes to help the children remember their names and properties.

Share different graphs representing the same data to compare and contrast the alternative ways of showing information.

 Take photos of the children's responses and methods for solving a problem. How did different children approach the same problem? Discuss the differences as a class and talk about misconceptions.

Modern foreign languages

 A day in the life: take photos to show a typical school day. Children can role play and freeze frame if necessary. Add text in the chosen language to describe each part of the day. If possible, add audio of children speaking in the foreign language.

PSHE

 Share 'hard-hitting' images to promote discussion with the class. Create a video showing children that are suffering, rainforests being destroyed or areas of drought – what do the children think about these images? What can be done about such problems?

 Share different facial expressions and examples of body language. What do they mean? What are the clues? As a class discuss the reasons why people have these emotions, how we can tell and how we can help them.

Science

 Record photographically an investigation, e.g. how a plant grows in different conditions. Add text to explain what is happening at each stage of the investigation and use the slideshow to present the findings.

 Compare the results and findings of different groups carrying out the same experiments. For example, after growing plants, groups could take photographs to see which has grown best – not only the tallest but also the one with the most leaves.

Taking things further

When adding audio, you may have the option to upload your own recording – this could be the children speaking into a microphone as an MP3 (see the audio section in Chapter 7). Using this technique, children can create their own advert or persuasive broadcast. The audio commentary plays as the photos scroll through.

Useful tips and resources

Some sites do not allow photos to be edited after they have been uploaded, so rotate or crop images before doing so.

Animoto provides an educational license at www.animoto.com/education. When the children wish to use Animoto, they register an account and include that code. This will allow them to make videos that are longer than 30 seconds without paying for the full license.

Online drawing tools

Getting started

Although there is usually a painting package installed on a computer, such as Microsoft Paint, it is also useful to explore other tools. Some must be installed, but there is a growing number of paint and art packages available online.

Sumo Paint (www.sumopaint.com) can be accessed without registering and an account created. Images can be saved online, downloaded and saved to the computer, or emailed to an account without the children needing an email address themselves. To begin, users can choose to upload an image from the computer, start with a blank canvas or choose an image from the Sumo gallery. There is a variety of familiar tools such as pencils, paint brushes and shapes, as well as more advanced tools such as layers. Sumo Paint also provides a range of filters to distort and blur the image.

Picozu (www.picozu.com) is a similar site that also includes shapes and layers.

More ideas

Other, similar, online drawing tools are listed below.

Canvastic – http://canvastic.net This site does not provide any shapes or layers but does offer a range of brushes, colours and a simple blank canvas.

Draw.to – http://draw.to Provides a small canvas on which to draw. When an image is complete users can press 'share' to create a **URL**, making it easy to share with others.

FlockDraw – http://flockdraw.com Enables the user to take painting a bit further. When the first user starts drawing, he/she is given a unique URL. If this is shared with others, multiple users can draw on the same canvas, creating possibilities for collaborative art.

Odosketch – http://sketch.odopod.com A basic site providing a range of pastel colours to create images.

Pencil Madness – http://pencilmadness.com Has a range of drawing effects.

Queeky – www.queeky.com/app A very similar feel to Sumo Paint but is more advanced than many other sites serving a similar purpose.

ScribblerToo – www.zefrank.com/scribbler/scribblertoo/ A simple drawing tool with no shapes or advanced features.

Sketchpad – http://mudcu.be/sketchpad/ Seems like a relatively basic tool at first glance but contains a huge array of tools and effects.

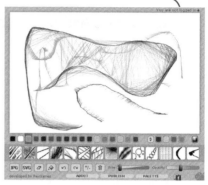

An online art tool in Pencil Madness.

One-minute artwork

Getting started

Some online tools allow users to turn their photographs into works of art in the style of famous artists. Others turn photographs into posters or apply effects with just a few clicks. This section explores some of these tools.

This is how these websites work:

1. Upload a photograph by browsing through your computer.
2. Select from the options or add additional text.
3. View the finished photograph.
4. Download it to your computer.

Examples of such sites include:

Hockneyizer – http://bighugelabs.com/hockney.php Turns a photograph into a picture made up of a range of Polaroids.

A range of shots produced using Hockneyizer.

Tiltshift – http://tiltshiftmaker.com/ Applies an effect that makes a photo appear to have shrunken elements. This turns the picture into a model village-style photograph.

PhotoVisi www.photovisi.com/ – Creates a mosaic of uploaded photographs.

PopArt – http://bighugelabs.com/popart.php Allows users to create Andy Warhol-style images.

The website BigHugeLabs (www.bighugelabs.com) is home to many of these quick photo-editing tools and provides an excellent opportunity for children to explore different ways of using their images.

There is also an education version of BigHugeLabs and this is free to sign up to. Once enrolled, the teacher can provide logins for children which will remove all adverts from the site.

Andy Warhol-style image using PopArt.

In the classroom

Art

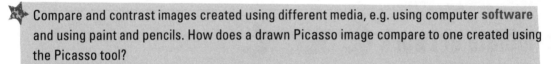 Compare and contrast images created using different media, e.g. using computer **software** and using paint and pencils. How does a drawn Picasso image compare to one created using the Picasso tool?

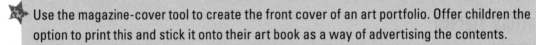 Use the magazine-cover tool to create the front cover of an art portfolio. Offer children the option to print this and stick it onto their art book as a way of advertising the contents.

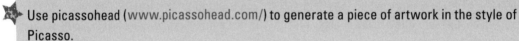 Use picassohead (www.picassohead.com/) to generate a piece of artwork in the style of Picasso.

Geography

 Use the map tool to show places that children have been or are going to. Discuss different climates, the equator and tropical regions to broaden their view of the world.

Literacy

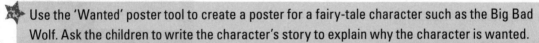 Use the 'Wanted' poster tool to create a poster for a fairy-tale character such as the Big Bad Wolf. Ask the children to write the character's story to explain why the character is wanted.

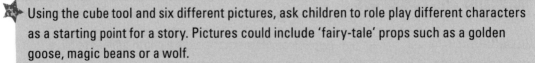 Using the cube tool and six different pictures, ask children to role play different characters as a starting point for a story. Pictures could include 'fairy-tale' props such as a golden goose, magic beans or a wolf.

Use the magazine-cover tool to give summaries of stories. For example, create a gossip-style magazine to tell the shocking tale of Goldilocks or Cinderella.

Music

 Record music created by the class, then use the CD-cover creator to make a cover representing the music. Promote this to parents as a possible way of raising school funds.

Science

 Use the jigsaw tool to explain a scientific process. The children have to piece it back together and explain what is happening. Why is the ice melting? How is the plant growing?

Whole school

 Create photo-based posters for school events, e.g. for an end-of-year drama production the poster could be in the style of a movie poster with credits displaying the names of the actors.

Taking things further

BeFunky – www.befunky.com Does not cost anything to get started but additional effects, such as adding **clipart**-style images, need a subscription registration. There is, however, a wide range of free materials and tools on the site, including converting the image into a pointillism-style picture or into an oil painting.

Photovisi – www.photovisi.com Can be used to create a mosaic or collage of images. Simply upload images to the site and choose a layout.

Tag Galaxy – www.taggalaxy.de Another site that collects images based around a particular search term or **tag**. It searches Flickr (www.flickr.com) for a particular term and shows the related images as a planet. Then it shows smaller planets with associated words orbiting the main search term. For example, if Queen Victoria was the key term, orbiting around the search word would be planets containing the words 'England', 'statue' and 'ship'. Clicking one of these brings up further connected searches. Clicking the main planet displays the images connected to the term.

Tuxpi – www.tuxpi.com Provides a range of tools for framing or recolouring your photograph. For example, users can upload a picture and convert it into black and white or sepia for a history project.

Useful tips and resources

When signing up to the BigHugeLabs Education version, you need to provide proof that you are a teacher. It usually takes a few days after this for the education license to be approved.

Most of the sites mentioned here allow the images to be downloaded or saved to the computer. If this is not the case and you would like to use the image later, you can take a screenshot to save the picture (remember to reference the site though).

Green-screen

Getting started

Green-screening (or chromakey) is the name given to a technique used to take a photograph against a coloured background before using computer software to alter the background. This is often used in film-making to add special effects. Using green-screening with videos is possible (see Chapter 8) but an ideal place to start is using photographs.

A range of software can be used to achieve these effects; Paint.NET™ is good as it is free. To download Paint.NET™, visit http://getpaint.net. You need two images to get started – one of the background and one of the character you wish to have in the foreground.

To create a green-screen style image using Paint.NET™, follow these simple steps:

Ensure that you have a background image.	
Get a picture of the person(s) you wish to have in the image. Think about their stance and positioning and how they will fit within the final composite image.	
Open the photo of the person in PaintNET™ and select the Magic Wand Tool. Set the tolerance level to approximately 25 and then click on a part of the blue or green background. The tolerance level may need to be adjusted.	
When a large majority of the background is selected, press the Delete key to remove it. Repeat the process until all the background colour has been removed. Click Edit, then select the whole image and Copy it.	

Open the background image in PaintNET™. Click Edit and then Paste New Layer.

The person will now be on the background but may be a different size. Find a corner of the image and drag this to resize as needed.

Save the final image.

In the classroom

Geography

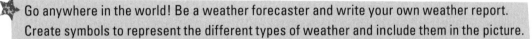
Go anywhere in the world! Be a weather forecaster and write your own weather report. Create symbols to represent the different types of weather and include them in the picture.

Travel to different climates. Wear appropriate clothes for the chosen climate to make the photo more realistic.

Shrink to become part of a volcano diagram, pointing out the different parts of the volcano.

History

Become an explorer and go inside an Egyptian pyramid or outside an Aztec temple.

Picture yourself with a famous person from history or in the time of a famous event, e.g. holidaying on the *Titanic* or talking to Winston Churchill about World War 2. What would you ask the famous person? What is it like to be on the *Titanic* as it sinks?

Literacy

Draw a scene from the story and become a character within your setting.

Become a news reporter at the scene of an event, e.g. a volcanic eruption or a protest march. Describe what is happening and what you can see.

Science

Travel to the moon or a different planet. Describe what it is like there. What can you see?

Travel to the bottom of the sea. Describe the setting and the wildlife around you.

Taking things further

Lighting is key to achieving better effects; it is easier to remove the background if it is all the same shade of blue/green. To do this, you may need to use a variety of lamps and lights to remove the shadows from the background. If you have a drama room or hall, use stage lighting to achieve this.

For more advanced use, read the section on green-screen videos in Chapter 8. This uses different software to create videos with alternative backgrounds.

Useful tips and resources

When taking a photograph of the character to appear on the chosen background image, you do not need to use specialist material or screens – blue or green fabric is enough. Green-screening may take a few attempts and some trial and error but the results are worth it, and children can learn a lot in the process.

To view some examples from Otter Class at Newhall Park Primary, visit http://bit.ly/greenscreenotter.

Google Art Project

Getting started

Built in the style of Google Street View, the Google Art Project (www. googleartproject.com) aims to bring the world's artistic masterpieces to everyone. There are two main aspects to this website: viewing artwork and touring museums. Using the Street View tools, users can 'walk' around the galleries of the world online. Over 150 museums are part of the project and over 30,000 pieces of art can be seen.

TOP TIP

The images in the Google Art Project are large, so bandwidth and **internet** speed may be an issue. Before using it with a whole class, test it on the teacher's computer or a machine that is networked rather than wireless.

Users can also search for a particular word or artist to find examples of his/her work. When these appear on screen, users can zoom in to see the high level of detail on each piece. Each image is also accompanied by details of the paints or oils used and information about the artist. Registration is in the form of a Google login and, once signed in, you can create your own online galleries to share with children.

In the classroom

Although the most obvious place for these resources is within an art lesson, the site has many other uses. It can be used as a research tool and is valuable for bringing lesser-known artists to the fore.

Art

 Create personal galleries that showcase different artistic elements such as line, colour or tone. Use these as the stimulus for children to draw similar images.

Before visiting an art gallery, explore certain pieces in the classroom.

Geography

 Use the Australian Rock Art collection to explore cave paintings and carvings. Discuss why the Australians drew on the caves and explore what the images could mean.

History

 Use images from throughout history to discuss the clothing, style and look of a particular time period.

Literacy

 Choose a picture and use this as the basis of a descriptive piece of writing. What is happening in the picture? Where is it? Who is involved?

 Use a piece of art as the basis for writing instructions. How was it created and put together?

 Write a leaflet about a gallery on the other side of the world, after you've visited it virtually.

PSHE

 Find a piece of art to match given emotions: anger, sadness, elation, calm, frustration, etc. Ask the children to create their own artwork to replicate these moods. What colours would evoke the image of anger or happiness?

Religious education

 The Jewish museums provide examples of religious artefacts that can be explored by the children and used to promote discussion about their possible uses.

More ideas

There are a number of other ways in which photographs can be used and edited within the classroom, including creating virtual tours or using pictures as an inspiration for a literacy activity.

> **Virtual Tour** – www.mapwing.com You can create a virtual tour of a particular room or building. This involves uploading a picture and creating hotspots with information. This could be used as a story with pictures of different scenes or to create a treasure trail with instructions and clues. A Mapwing account is needed in order to create your own tour.

Escape Motions – www.escapemotions.com/experiments.html A range of tools that provide different ways of drawing, including drawing with fire, oil or particles. Changing the sliders on each tool produces different effects to create new images.

Google Images – http://images.google.com Finding images to use within the classroom can sometimes be difficult, but Google's image search has a few helpful tools. After entering the search term, scroll down on the left-hand side to access these tools. Using the search term 'elephant' as an example, the tools can help to narrow down the results in several ways:

TOP TIP

In Escape Motions draw a quick image, such as a line, and then press save. This will usually provide a pop-up window. Agree to this and the site will reload. If this is done after the children have drawn their full image, it will reload the page and provide a blank screen, so it is better to do this when the site first loads.

1. **Colours** – Select a colour to find elephants that are purple or orange. There is also a black and white option which is useful if colour printing is restricted in the school.
2. **Clipart** – This removes photos and shows only the clipart-style images. Again, this helps to reduce printing costs as many of these images have very simple outlines.
3. **Size** – This is useful if the picture is being printed in a large format, and ensures that large pictures are found. Alternatively, if the picture is to be shared, then a smaller image may be more appropriate.
4. **Similar** – Once you have the results of your search, hover over an image that suits your purposes and choose 'Similar'. This function removes the pictures that bare no resemblance to the one chosen.

PicLits – www.piclits.com Choose a photo and add keywords to describe it. You can use the pre-selected words or add your own. This can then be displayed on the whiteboard as a starting point for a creative piece of writing or as a way of introducing more varied vocabulary. To save your PicLits, you will need to sign up to a free account.

More tips on searching for images can be found at www.undertenminutes.com/?p=263.

Another picture search tool is Picsearch (www.picsearch.com/) which will also provide a way for the children to search for images.

Please note, there may be restrictions on which images can be used and how they can be used. Check with the website that the image has been taken from before using images elsewhere. Google Image search has an Advanced Search option which can find images that are copyright free.

CHAPTER 6 FINDING THINGS OUT

Introduction

This chapter explores different ways of finding out information. It is important to remember that the **internet** contains a wealth of information but it is not all aimed at children. The majority of sites are for adults or those who can read at a higher level than the majority of children within primary schools. There are, however, a few tricks and tips to help younger children.

This chapter covers:

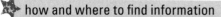

- how and where to find information
- what to do with information after finding it
- how to make games to help reinforce learning
- how to find different places around the world.

For many children, particularly in Key Stage 2, research will be an important part of their ICT curriculum. This will not happen exclusively within ICT lessons, but will also occur in History, Geography or topic lessons. The skills involved in finding information and researching are becoming increasingly important. Although books are available in school, a number of factors means that children sometimes use the internet rather than books to find the answers they need.

The main purposes of this chapter are to identify how to research and narrow down the results and also what to do with the information once it has been collected. How should children present it? Should they create a presentation or can they be allowed to choose other ways of sharing their learning with others?

Researching

Getting started

If children are asked to suggest a source of **online** information, they will invariably say Google first, with others such as Bing further down the list. Although Google (www.google.co.uk) is the most popular search engine in the world, it is important for the children to know how Google works, what features it has and how to find the information they want. Also, what the alternatives are.

When searching for online information with children, it is important that they begin to get a sense of whether the site will be useful to them or not. Some schools follow the TASK approach as outlined on the Parkfield ICT website (www.parkfieldict.co.uk/search/). When a website has been found, children should ask the following questions:

T – Title: Does the title look useful?

A – Author: Is the author trustworthy?

S – Summary: Does the content seem relevant?

K – Kids: Is the website aimed at children?

Not all of these questions can be answered for every site, but they do encourage children to think about the links they find in search results. If the class has a blog, then they will understand that anyone can post online and that not all of the information on the internet is true or correct. This should be compared with information books and the fact that content is verified before the book can be published.

It is also very important to show the children sites such as answers.com (www.answers.com), as these allow anyone to post questions and answers. Often children realise that they need to be wary of sites such as these as they can contain spelling and grammatical errors.

Google tips

Google has several features that can narrow down search results, the majority of which are on the left-hand side of the Google results page. Often when a search term is entered, there are a great number of results, so careful consideration about what is entered into the search box is essential. For example, searching for 'Victorian inventions' produces more accurate results than 'Victorians', but there are ways of further improving accuracy once the results are displayed. These include the following:

With the **location** settings, users can choose to see results from the UK only.

The **time** feature can help to narrow results to the most recent. Searching for items within the last week will bring up current news items rather than old stories.

Use the **More search tools** option to provide a range of other tools, including 'Related searches'.

Choosing **Sites with images** will show sites that contain images. Although this covers many webpages, it could be an indication that the sites are for a younger audience.

Changing the **Reading level** can help to remove the more advanced results that use technical vocabulary. Using the 'Basic' option will narrow this down even further.

Other search tools

The following search engines use a custom version of Google which helps to remove adverts and focusses the content on primary-aged children.

Search page on Infant Encyclopaddia

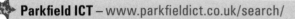

- **Parkfield ICT** – www.parkfieldict.co.uk/search/

- **Searchy Pants** – www.searchypants.com/

- **Primary Safe Search** – http://primaryschoolict.com/

- **Infant Encyclopaedia** – www.parkfieldict.co.uk/infant/ Created by Simon Haughton, provides simple information on a range of topics commonly taught within the infant classroom.

- **Qwiki** – www.qwiki.com Once a search term has been entered, the site produces a range of videos and supporting images with narration.

- **Wikipedia** – www.wikipedia.org Often the first site to appear in the majority of search results and it should not be ignored. It is useful to explain to children that Wikipedia is created with the help of thousands of people editing articles and, as such, there may be discrepancies and errors.

Presenting research

Getting started

When children are comfortable finding information online, how do they record it? More importantly, how do they share it with others?

Recording information

When recording information it is important to ensure that the children are taught how to take notes, to find the key points they need, and not simply copy down everything on the site. They should be shown, and allowed to choose from, a variety of different 'analogue' ways of note-taking, including blank pieces of paper, mind-maps and structured question-and-answer boxes.

Children need to understand that when they are finding and using information they must credit where the information, picture or video has come from. Children around Year 3 and Year 4 should be able to explain that they have found information from a particular website and, as children leave Key Stage 2, they should be happy adding links to their work to show the source of information.

Using and sharing information

There are many different ways in which research and information can be used. This may be as part of a topic or another piece of work such as a written report. The obvious way to present information is as part of a presentation, but below we explore some alternatives.

- **Crossword** – Use a site such as PuzzleMaker (www.puzzle-maker.com/) to create a crossword based on the information found. Print them out for others to complete.
- **Digital book** – Using one of the Digital Storytelling tools (see Chapter 2), ask the children to create a class reference book.
- **Game** – Ask children to use the information they have learned to create a game for others.
- **Mind-map** – Sort information into different areas and then create a mind-map of ideas. This could be accomplished using sites such as Prezi or Popplet (see Chapter 4).
- **Stickies** – Use a site such as Primary Wall (www.primarywall.com) to collect information and then sort it for others to read later.
- **Word cloud** – Write the information in note form or copy sentences from the site and paste them into a word cloud site such as Wordle (see Chapter 2).

Questions and answers

Getting started

An increasing number of tools are available online to create flashcards and games based on simple knowledge and recall. Although these may not require high-level skills or thought processes, simple question-and-answer games and puzzles are useful in many areas of the curriculum.

This is how these websites work:

1. Visit the website and choose the game type.
2. Enter a selection of questions and answers.
3. Assign the answers to the questions.
4. Either link to or embed the finished game in a blog or **VLE**.

These activities only take a few minutes to create and play, and provide a useful way of learning facts such as times tables, spellings or key dates. They can also be used to assess children's understanding. Use a multiple-choice quiz that

TOP TIP

These sites also have links to games created by other users, but they should always be tested and checked by the teacher before being used with the class.

has a range of answers from which to select; give it to children at the start of a lesson and again at the end to assess how much they have learned. Creating the games yourself means that content can be tailored to a particular class or group of children.

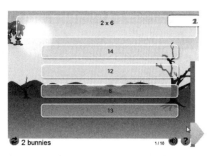

One of the advantages of sites such as What2Learn (www. what2learn.com) and Zondle (www.zondle.com) is that, due to their simplicity, children can also create games to share with each other. This benefits their own learning as they research and check the information before including it in the game. It requires higher-order thinking to choose different incorrect answers to make the game

One of the games available on Zondle.

more difficult for the player. Giving children the chance to make games also encourages discussion of 'good' questions and open/closed questions.

In the classroom

The games and activities can be used across the curriculum where there is a need for recalling facts and information. They can also be used in areas where children make common mistakes.

Cross-curricular

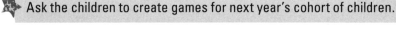
Ask the children to create games for next year's cohort of children.

Literacy

Use games and quizzes to find out how well the children have understood a piece of text.

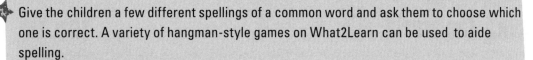
Give the children a few different spellings of a common word and ask them to choose which one is correct. A variety of hangman-style games on What2Learn can be used to aide spelling.

Give children a sentence with a missing word. Ask them to select the correct adjective/adverb/noun/verb from a list of options.

Maths

Provide a number sentence with a missing number, and get the children to choose the answer that completes the sum.

Match the name of a shape to a description of its properties. Discuss which shape has four right-angles or internal angles that equal 180 degrees.

Modern foreign languages

 Match words in the target language to their English equivalents.

Science

 Give the children multiple answers to a scientific problem and challenge them to choose the correct answer.

Taking things further

Other tools allowing you to create a game or activity within seconds include:

Hangman – www.webhangman.com/hangman.php Select the two-player game to play with the class. The first player enters a word and the second tries to guess what the word is.

Wordsearch Maker – www.wordsearchmaker.net Use this website to create word searches to help practise spellings.

Useful tips and resources

Quiz!

An anagram game that can be created on www.what2learn.com.

Pete Richardson has blogged about Zondle within the classroom (http://primarypete.net/?s=zondle). There is also a guide to setting up user accounts for Zondle on the Under Ten Minutes site (www.undertenminutes.com/?s=zondle).

Mapping the world

Getting started

When using maps with a group or class, Google Maps (www.google.com/maps) is invaluable. The maps are extremely detailed and kept reasonably up to date. With the addition of Street View, users can also 'walk' around the locations on the majority of maps. Photographs can be viewed from a range of places on the map by dragging the small yellow man onto the map and placing him on any circle. Having the majority of the world at the click of a mouse means that children can explore global landmarks.

This is how Google Maps works:

1. Users enter a place name or post code.

TOP TIP

Under Ten Minutes (www.undertenminutes.com/?tag=google-maps) has a video explaining how to create a map to support a topic area.

2. They choose whether to use map view or satellite to see a photo of the area.
3. They can zoom and move around to find out more.

Text bubble for a location on Google Maps.

Making a map

Users of Google Maps can also create their own maps. This does not mean that they will be inventing new countries, but simply producing a set of pins or markers that will overlay onto the world map.

For some examples of user-created maps, try the Castle Map (http://bit.ly/castlemap) or the Houses and Homes map (http://bit.ly/housesandhomes), both designed to highlight different locations around the UK to support topics in Key Stage 1.

 A Google **login** is needed in order to make a map. After logging in, visit Google Maps and under the My Places tab, there is the option to create a new map. When this has been done, any items that are searched for can be saved to the new map.

 The publicity settings can be changed so that the map can be seen by others.

 When a marker on the map is clicked, a speech bubble appears. This can contain text, links and images and can be used as a way for the children to add further information.

In the classroom

For ways of using maps to tell stories check out Chapter 2. For other subject areas, see below.

Art

 Using Street View, find examples of homes or buildings in different countries. Ask the children to replicate these using a different medium.

Cross-curricular

 Use Street View to discuss potential hazards on a school trip. Show the children an image of the road they will cross and what to look out for. They could even write their own risk assessment.

 Use the MOLE (map of outdoor learning experiences) (http://bit.ly/molemap) to look for locations for potential school trips.

★ Ask the children to use the speech bubble tools on various locations, to write a brief history of their life.

★ Ask children to use the speech bubbles to create a video advert designed to persuade people to visit a particular place.

Geography

★ Ask children to create a profile of different mountains, rivers or capital cities around the world. Where are they? How long/big are they?

★ With the children, look at a physical map showing a capital city. Ask them to step into the map using Street View and compare this with the physical map.

★ Although Google Maps does not provide Ordnance Survey information, it is available on Bing Maps (www.bing.com/maps).

Literacy

★ Write directions for travelling from one place to another. The children could explore the world, following clues and instructions until they reach a chosen destination.

★ Find out more about a book by exploring the place in which it was set. For example, discuss the different areas in which Roald Dahl, in his book *Boy*, grew up.

Maths

★ Using the measurement tool, ask the children to find out how far away they live from school. Compare the difference between the actual distance they travel and the distance 'as the crow flies'.

★ Use the measurement tool to work out the area and perimeter of different places.

★ Use Maths Maps (http://edte.ch/blog/maths-maps/) to answer questions about different areas.

Taking things further

Use Animaps (www.animaps.com) to create an animated map. There are a number of showcases on the site to show how Animaps can work. As the characters/icons move across the map, pop-up bubbles or pictures can be displayed, adding an extra dimension to narrative text.

CHAPTER 7 SOUND AND MUSIC

Introduction

When it comes to teaching, enthusiasm for a subject often depends on teacher confidence, and music is no exception. This chapter provides ideas on how to use audio in the classroom, as well as references to websites and tools that can help children to create music.

This chapter covers:

- a range of tools to make music and compose audio
- editing audio files.
- creating podcasts

The majority of these tools give children the chance to experiment with sounds and instruments that they may not normally have access to. An additional benefit is that, with the use of headphones, the children can all be 'playing' different instruments at the same time without giving you a headache!

Equipment

- Headphones: these do not need to be particularly expensive.
- Microphones: useful for recording audio directly into the computer. For most uses, an inexpensive **USB** microphone will be fine; if there is a need for a higher-quality recording it may be worth investing more. For more about microphones see page 11.

Composition and sequencing

Simple tools

Tools that do not necessarily use 'real' instruments are a great place for less confident music teachers to start. Generally, these tools simply require some dragging and dropping to begin the music. There is often not a way to export the music but the tools provide an opportunity for the children to experiment and create music in an unthreatening way.

- Project Two (http://bit.ly/projecttwo), Circuli (http://bit.ly/circuli), Otomata (www.bit.ly/otomata), BallDroppings (http://bit.ly/balldropping), Lullatone (http://bit.ly/lullatone) and Inudge (www.inudge.net) all feature the option to click or drag to create very simple noises using icons or graphics.

A suitable tool to begin with is Isle of Tune (www. isleoftune.com) which starts with a blank field on which children draw a road and then add trees and buildings. Each piece of scenery has a different sound attached to it, then, when a car is added to the road, the notes are combined to create music.

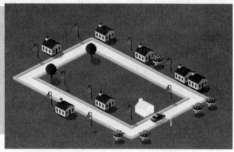

An example of the 'score' from the Isle of Tune.

More advanced tools

The tools described in this section are more advanced in the way that the music is composed. These often use real instruments and clips of music rather than just sounds and noises. These can be added together to create a piece of music. Not all the sites enable you to **download** the finished audio track – many publish the track **online**, and others provide a link to play the music on the website instead.

This is how these websites work:

1. Students are presented with a timeline to represent their piece of music – this may have different layers or instruments playing at once.
2. Using the library of clips, select some audio and drag it onto the timeline.
3. Edit the audio by rearranging the clips or changing the length.
4. Publish the finished track.

If there are Apple devices available in school, such as a Mac or iPad, give children the opportunity to use Garageband (www.apple.com/ilife/garageband/) **software** to create their musical masterpiece. This is also a tool that offers real instruments and the option of layering the sound to create the final track.

Useful tips and resources

Soundation (http://soundation.com/studio), Aviary (www.aviary.com/) and JamStudio (www.jamstudio. com/Studio/index.htm) all provide a bank of sounds for children to use when creating their track.

Using audio in the classroom

Getting started

There are many ways in which audio and music can be used in the classroom: sometimes this involves using clips that have been recorded elsewhere; on other occasions the children record it themselves.

In the classroom

History

 Pretend that you have teleported back in time to be on a boat in the Spanish Armada or you are a slave in Egypt. Conduct an interview with the people that you meet.

ICT

 Tools like PowerPoint® or ZooBurst would benefit from audio narration. Record the audio, edit it and then **upload** it to narrate the story.

Record the instructions for your 2Do It Yourself game (see Chapter 9). These could play when the title screen loads. Sounds could also be used when the game is over, the character is caught or when items are collected.

Literacy

 Record instructions for simple tasks. Children can then listen and see if they can follow the instructions. For example, give instructions for drawing a shape that consists of four or five other simple shapes. As the instructions are played, children should attempt to draw the shape. Discuss how difficult it is to follow instructions without visual clues.

Maths

 Rap about maths (http://bit.ly/mathsraps) – perhaps about times tables or how to divide large numbers.

Science

 Create a song to help remember key concepts, e.g. the water cycle, or to remember the names of the planets.

Whole school and cross-curricular

 Use a countdown timer (http://classtools.net/education-games-php/timer/) to encourage the children to pack away quickly, get changed for PE or line up.

 Create a weekly radio podcast. This could be an interview with the school council, teachers or other people within the school.

Taking things further

Audioboo (www.audioboo.com) or Vocaroo (www.vocaroo.com) are good places to store audio files. Simply visit the website, record the audio and save. These recordings can then be embedded into a **blog** or website.

Useful tips and resources

When creating audio files, search tools to find clips of music that can be downloaded are useful. FindSounds (www.findsounds.com) and SoundFX Now (http://soundfxnow.com) both enable the children to download clips and sound effects to enhance their music or audio recordings.

Editing audio

TOP TIP

Videos offering guidance for editing audio with Audacity can be found on Under Ten Minutes (www.undertenminutes.com).

Getting started

To record audio, the children need a microphone and the ability to transfer sound to the computer. Most microphones provide the ability to record directly into the computer as a .wav or **MP3** file. Once the audio is on the computer, it can be treated like many other files and be moved or edited as required.

There are a number of tools available to edit audio but the most popular tends to be Audacity (http://audacity.sourceforge.net/). This is a simple, free download that provides a timeline for the children. The children basically import their audio and can edit the recording by trimming either end, remove silences and import other sound effects too, as shown in the table below.

Once imported, it is clear from the timeline where the audio is playing and where it is silent.	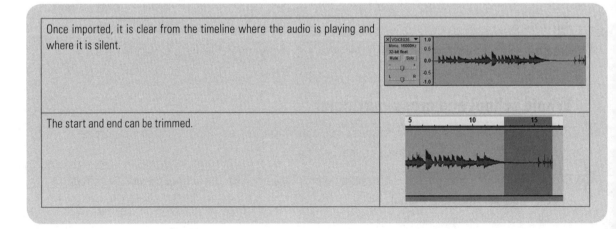
The start and end can be trimmed.	

Silences can be removed by highlighting and removing them.	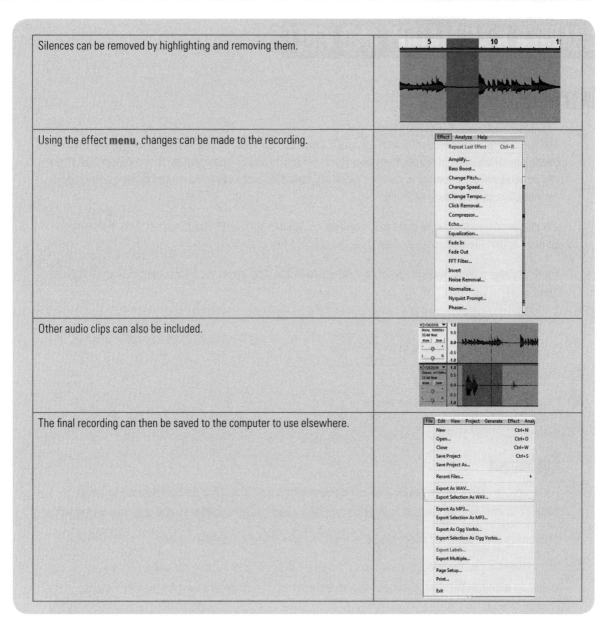
Using the effect **menu**, changes can be made to the recording.	
Other audio clips can also be included.	
The final recording can then be saved to the computer to use elsewhere.	

Taking things further

To save the Audacity recording as an MP3 file, you need to install the Lame MP3 **plugin**. Instructions for doing this can be found at http://bit.ly/mp3lame.

CHAPTER 8

CHAPTER 8 ANIMATION AND VIDEO

Introduction

The focus of this chapter is the way in which video can be shot, edited and used within the primary classroom for a variety of different purposes. It is becoming easier (and cheaper) to record video and this can be achieved on a number of devices including dedicated video cameras, digital cameras and mobile devices such as iPod Touch or iPads.

It is also becoming simpler to store video **online**, using sites such as YouTube, so that recorded video can be used within the classroom or shared on the school **blog** or website.

There are many other ways in which to use video in the classroom, and this chapter also addresses those.

This chapter covers:

 how video can be used within the classroom

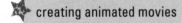 creating animated movies

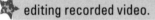 recording the screen to assist learning

editing recorded video.

Equipment

To complete many of the tasks you will need a video camera. This does not need to be a dedicated camera, as long as it enables you to record a video and transfer it to the computer.

Webcams are useful for recording the pictures to create animation pages.

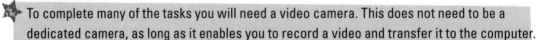 When working with video, a powerful computer is beneficial. Video files are often very large, so a computer that is connected to the **network**, rather than a wireless device, is recommended.

There may be issues with the format of the recorded video – your device may have settings that can be changed to ensure that it will work as required.

Using video in the classroom

Getting started

Although the majority of videos mentioned here will be online, there is no need to **upload** every video that is recorded. Many teachers find it easier to record parts of their lesson or the children's learning and share this back either with the class or as part of an assembly.

This could include:

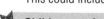 Children performing a poem, reading stories or any other speaking opportunity.

 Drama performances and role play within literacy lessons.

 PE lessons – focusing on positioning, form and performance.

YouTube

Videos on YouTube are freely available. However, be aware that, although there is a wealth of material available on YouTube, many schools have this site blocked. YouTube has a 'Copyright School' that teaches about copyright and the use of video (www.youtube.com/t/copyright_education). It is well worth investigating the YouTube for Schools feature (www.youtube.com/schools).

Other sites

The two main places to look for free videos are TeacherTube (www.teachertube.com) and the BBC Learning Zone (www.bbc.co.uk/learningzone/clips/). The BBC site showcases clips from a range of BBC shows including short clips from shows such as *Bang Goes the Theory* and *Frozen Planet*. One site to help with Literacy videos is the Literacy Shed (www.literacyshed.com).

In the classroom

Design technology

Use video to engage and enthuse about a specific topic. The video at http://bit.ly/ thecardboard shows children how one boy's DT project became world famous.

History

Watch clips from recent history.

Use clips from *Horrible Histories* (www.bbc.co.uk/cbbc/shows/horrible-histories) to help bring history to life.

Literacy

Use Mr Thorne and Geraldine Giraffe on YouTube, offering over 300 videos to support the teaching of phonics (www.mrthorne.com/).

Find videos of poets performing their own poems, such as Michael Rosen's 'Chocolate Cake' (http://bit.ly/rosencake).

Maths

For more able mathematicians, the Numberphile channel (www.youtube.com/Numberphile) shows a range of videos covering some advanced aspects of maths.

Use videos to highlight numeracy misconceptions, e.g. http://bit.ly/13x7is28.

Videos can be used for counting. Try http://bit.ly/countin5s.

There are many opportunities to use videos and animations with younger children. The video at http://bit.ly/theshapesong is useful when learning about 2D shapes.

PE

Show videos of different activities either as part of a warm up or to highlight form and performance. Examples could include the New Zealand Haka or watching a hockey game.

Show dance routines to recent songs and try to copy them. Then make up some of your own.

Science

Use channels such as Steve Spangler's Science (www.youtube.com/user/SteveSpanglerScience) to show experiments that are sometimes hard to replicate in the classroom.

For sharing videos about space, try Deep Sky (www.youtube.com/DeepSkyVideos).

Songs are a great way of helping children to remember facts. Learn these songs as a class to present in an assembly (http://bit.ly/solarsong; http://bit.ly/thewatercycle).

Whole school

Teachers can refer to the TEDTalks and TED-Ed (www.youtube.com/user/TEDtalksDirector and www.youtube.com/user/TEDEducation) that showcase talks and presentations from a range of speakers and a selection of education-based videos.

Taking things further

Schools wishing to collate all their videos in one place can sign up to create a YouTube channel. This can be linked on the school website. An example of this is at www.youtube.com/user/stjohnswaltham.

Useful tips and resources

Rob Smith blogs about useful videos for the primary classroom (http://teacher-rob.posterous.com/).

Animations

Getting started

Creating animations inspires creativity in many children. After being shown the basics in the classroom many attempt to create their own animations, and it is useful for them to be able to share these with their peers.

There are generally three different types of animation **software**:

1. Stop-frame animation – models are created and then the software takes a picture. The models are then moved slightly and another picture taken. This is repeated and the images are put together to create a video.
2. Image animation – allows users to draw pictures on each frame. The frames are then composed together to make the finished movie.
3. Pre-made graphics – tools where users are given a variety of characters, backgrounds and features with which to create their animations.

Stop-frame animation

Creating stop-frame animation is a long process and can be frustrating. Some software, such as JellyCam (www.jellycam.co.uk), can be used online. For the best results it is worth buying software such as Zu3D (www.zu3d.com/) or I Can Animate (www.kudlian.net/products/icananimate/).

Image animation

Tools such as 2Animate (www.2simple.com/2animate/), Doink (www.doink.com), ABCya (www.abcya.com/animate.htm) and Pivot Stick-Man Animator (http://bit.ly/pivotstickman) provide a facility to draw pictures and add these to frames, usually based on a timeline. These images are then combined to create an animated movie.

Pivot Stick-Man allows users to create simple stick-men and animate them.

Pre-made graphics

A number of tools provide a selection of pre-made characters to animate and these generally require a **login**. Examples include Go! Animate (www.goanimate.com), Fluxtime (www.fluxtime.com), Xtranormal (www.xtranormal.com) and Dvolver (www.dvolver.com). Movements can be given to characters and text added to create the movie. These moves tend to be fairly short but some websites enable the children to embed the videos onto a blog or website afterwards.

In the classroom

Design technology

 Take photos as a model is constructed and play them back to watch the model build itself.

Geography

 Create an animated volcano to show what happens when it erupts. Apply a similar idea to erosion or other natural occurrences.

History

 Retell a Greek myth using models. Think about the characters and the setting.

 Re-enact a historic event such as the Great Fire of London.

Literacy

 Animate a story using plasticine models. This works well with traditional tales as the audience is likely to know the basis of the story.

Maths

 Write a problem on the whiteboard. Take pictures of the problem-solving process to help others solve it.

Music

 Use the Pivot Stick-Man tool to create a new dance routine for a chosen song.

PSHE

 Enact a scenario, such as an incident of bullying, to provoke discussion among the children.

Science

 Animate a scientific concept such as blood moving around the body, food being digested or the water cycle.

Whole school

 Create an animated school prospectus or tour to share with visitors to the school website.

Useful tips and resources

If you plan to create stop-frame animations it is worth being aware of what is meant by frames per second (fps). Usually a film will have 24fps to ensure the animation is smooth and realistic. I Can Animate (www. kudlian.net) allows this to be adjusted and usually starts with 12fps. This means that for just one second of movie, children need to take 12 pictures, something they will need to consider while making their film. Some examples of animations created by children can be found at http://bit.ly/class8animation.

Green-screen videos

Getting started

Moving on from taking photographs and adding green-screen effects is the use of green-screen video. This can be challenging as lighting becomes even more important when people are moving and there are shadows to consider. High-quality videos can be achieved much more easily on a Mac (using iMovie) than on a PC. Generally, the free software available for the PC will not achieve results of as high a quality as paid-for software. Wax 2.0e (www.debugmode.com/wax/) is among the best free tools available.

This is how these tools work:

1. Record the children performing in front of a green/blue screen.
2. Import the video into the software.
3. Select the background.
4. Remove the background and replace with an alternative such as a rainforest or the moon.

In the classroom

Green-screen videos work well when children are stationary, for example as part of a news report or bulletin.

TOP TIP

Check whether the software you are using will need a blue or green background or whether it can cope with both.

Geography

 Report on a volcanic eruption, earthquake or similar event. Explain how the disaster was caused and the effect it had on the people living nearby.

History

 Report on a historic event such as the Great Fire of London, the end of World War 2 or the Queen's Jubilee. Use images of these events in the background while reading the news report.

Literacy

 Present a news report from the home of a fairy-tale character.

Religious education

 Create a puppet show based on the nativity.

Useful tips and resources

Green-screen videos can be very difficult to achieve, particularly on a PC with only free software available. A blog post about the experience is at http://bit.ly/iangreenblog.

Editing video

The timeline on Movie-Maker®.

Sometimes a video has been recorded and needs to be edited, e.g. trimming the start or end of the video. The main video-editing tool on a PC is Windows Movie-Maker® which is already installed on the computer. On a Mac, iMovie is included as standard.

For those with a Google account, there is the option on YouTube to edit videos before uploading them. The site (www.youtube.com/create) offers a range of tools to either remix the video, trim and crop the clip or animate from scratch. These tools are free but there may be a charge for additional features.

This is how Movie-Maker® works:

1. Import the video into Movie-Maker®.
2. Add extra pictures as necessary.
3. Export the video for use later.
4. Drag the video onto the timeline.
5. Include title sequences and credits.

The final video can be watched or uploaded online. It is also possible to combine videos to make a longer film.

CHAPTER 9 GAME DESIGN, CONTROL AND PROGRAMMING

Introduction

When IT was first introduced to the classroom, a strong emphasis was placed on the need for programming. This was due to the tools at hand, but also because many of the computer games played by young children had been typed and coded using the same machines. As computers and games have developed in complexity, it has become harder to include programming within the primary classroom. Children may lack motivation to make a rudimentary game compared with the Xbox-style visuals many are used to at home. However, there has been a recent push towards the inclusion of programming and basic computer science as a key part of the ICT curriculum. This chapter introduces some of the tools to facilitate this.

The chapter also considers different websites that teach the basics of control technology, which in its simplest form involves moving an object from A to B but can also involve completing a task. Control technology combines well with programming and game design as it involves sets of instructions that need to be written (or programmed) and then tested. Once tested, they may need to be refined or changed completely.

The majority of game-design tools available are of a graphical nature, offering pictorial tools and icons to enable the user to get started. Some lines of code may be involved, but can be tackled by the more advanced user (these tools are covered in 'More ideas', page 81).

This chapter covers:

- moving characters around mazes, considering instructions and sequences
- creating games using simple drag-and-drop-style tools
- creating interactive worlds with more depth and control.

Encourage the children to answer 'What if …?' questions when they are programming as this helps them to become not only problem-solvers but also problem creators. Game design challenges children and teachers, but it is also incredibly inspiring.

You do not need to know how every aspect of a piece of **software** works or what every line of code will do. However it is useful to be able to make a simple game where a character performs a straightforward task, such as moving from A to B. Programming, above almost all other aspects of ICT, lends itself well to the approach of letting children explore for themselves the different possibilities. Collect ideas and new discoveries and perhaps display them in the classroom. Invite the children to present their findings to the rest of the class using the interactive whiteboard.

A-maze-ing instructions

A BeeBot

Getting started

Programming and control in primary schools usually begins with 'floor robots' such as Roamers or BeeBots. These tend to be used mainly in Reception and Year 1 where the children experiment with moving the robot from one area of the classroom to another. Preceding this, children may have acted out 'controlling' each other in the playground, asking their friend to move 'three steps to the left'. The main teaching aspects involved when using these tools are directions and distance, e.g. measuring the length the robot has travelled.

This is how floor robots work:

1. Clear the previous program, usually using a CM (Clear Memory) button.
2. Choose which direction to send the robot in.
3. Choose a distance (the unit of measurement for floor robots is usually one body length).
4. Add additional sequences if needed, e.g. left turn, then forward 4.
5. Press Go.
6. Repeat or refine the program as required.

Children can progress quickly from planning a simple route forward to including turns and more complex routines. They should be encouraged to predict where they think the robot will finish. If their prediction is not accurate give them the opportunity to discuss how to change the sequence in order to complete the task.

In the classroom

Although the main purpose of these robots is to introduce basic programs, movements and controlling devices, there are other ways in which they can be used as a cross-curricular tool.

Cross-curricular

 Prepare a multiple-choice quiz. Arrange two areas on the floor: 'A' and 'B'. Split the class into teams depending on how many BeeBots you have available. Read out a question with a choice of two answers. Teams must move their BeeBots to the area that corresponds to the correct answer.

Geography

 Draw a simple road map or map of the classroom on large paper and place on the floor.

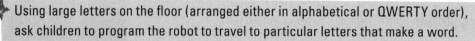

Program the BeeBot to move around it on a journey.

Literacy

⭐ Using large letters on the floor (arranged either in alphabetical or QWERTY order), ask children to program the robot to travel to particular letters that make a word.

⭐ Use pictures to show parts of a story. Children take it in turns to control the robot to reach each picture. When the robot arrives at the picture, the children tell that part of the story.

Maths

⭐ Main teaching points revolve around the use of directions and angles. For example, on the Roamer each turn is measured in degrees, so the children need to understand that 90 degrees is required to make a left or right turn.

⭐ Provide the children with a large shape, such as a rectangle, and ask them to plan a set of instructions to move the robot around the perimeter of the shape.

⭐ Investigate the instructions needed to make the robots travel in the shape of regular polygons. Link this work to a discussion about internal and external angles.

⭐ Provide a large grid to combine work with coordinates. Can the children get the robot to A5 or B2?

Online games

After programming the robots, the next step is usually an on-screen representation of this activity; perhaps using the Roamer **software**, the BeeBot **app** or something else. A variety of similar tools **online** help to promote problem-solving, thinking ahead and strategy. Some are listed below and can be found on the ICT Planning website (www.ictplanning.co.uk). These games can be played individually but generally work well when played with a partner as they give children the opportunity to discuss their ideas.

LabRat – Using the arrow keys on the keyboard directs the rat around the maze.

LightBot – The purpose of this game is to get the robot to light up when he reaches the blue squares.

Rommy the Robot – Another maze game, but the robot must be sequenced before the go button is pressed. This is very similar to the floor-robot style control and encourages children to plan their route before they begin.

A LightBot Maze

A floormat for a BeeBot/Roamer.

Taking things further

For smaller floor robots, design a mat or surface for them to explore. This could be a town, a forest or a new planet. Ask the children to design different aspects of the setting and then control the robot to travel around it.

For more advanced floor robot use, consider using the Pro-Bots, which allow the children to use numbers in their programs.

Drag-and-drop game design

Getting started

TOP TIP

For examples of the potential of 2DIY, visit the 2DIY Archive (www.2diyarchive.co.uk) created by Simon Widdowson.

One of the simplest game-design tools available to schools is 2Do It Yourself (or 2DIY) available from 2Simple software (www.2simple.com). 2DIY provides a range of templates in which to create different sorts of games. This starts with simple activities that allow the children to drag and drop objects onto the screen. It also includes activities requiring the children to match pairs. The games export as Flash files (.swf) making them ideal for sharing online or on a **blog**.

Beyond these simple activities is a range of other game templates such as platform games or maze games. Using this software, a simple game can be created in seconds, and additional elements can be added to create games with more depth. The children can draw the characters and objects, use the **clipart** library or import pictures that they have saved or **downloaded**.

When creating these games, there are several elements that can be altered:

The main character. To move him around, use the arrow keys (the keys used to control the character can be changed if necessary).	
The apples represent objects to collect. These may be animated and can be worth differing numbers of points.	
These are the monsters that will try and harm the main character. The game can be set so that the main character loses a life or loses points.	

The brick tool. Whatever is painted into this area will replicate on all bricks throughout the level.

Images courtesy of Tim Bleazard.

In the classroom

Art

 Use the jigsaw tool to piece together an example of artwork produced by a famous artist.

 Draw characters for the game and scan them. Use the import tool to add them to the game.

Design technology

Ask the children to create packaging for a game they have designed. What images and words do they want to include on it? How could they persuade people to buy their game instead of the others available?

Geography

 Label different countries, cities or features on an imported map.

History

 Use the labelling tool to label parts of a roman soldier or timeline.

 Use the cloze procedure to assess knowledge on a given subject.

 Use the platform game or catching game to create a game where you collect artefacts from a certain time period.

Literacy

 Use the drag tool to drag shapes onto the screen to create characters. Use these as the basis of a story. The shapes can be adjusted and rearranged to create a composite image.

 Using the levels function, create an interactive story with up to ten pages. The main characters can make their way through the levels (story) completing tasks and moving the story forward as needed. Text can also be included on each page.

Maths

- Use the pairs activity to match equivalent fractions, multiples or questions and answers.
- Using the collection tool, collect multiples of a particular number, ignoring the incorrect answers.
- Use the sequencing activity to put times or numbers in order.

Modern foreign languages

- Use the voice recording on the pairs activity to match English words with those in a particular foreign language.
- Create a matching game to link vocabulary written in another language with the English equivalent.

Science

- Use the labelling tool to label a diagram, e.g. parts of a plant or the water cycle.
- Create a healthy eating game using the collecting tool. Collect the images of healthy food and ignore the sweets that come your way!

Whole school

- Create a sequencing activity based around the school day. Ask the children to put the pictures into the correct order.

Taking things further

By right-clicking on the Play button, some simple code is displayed. This is an excellent way of showing children how code can be implemented within a game. The numbers can be adjusted to change how high, or how quickly, the character jumps and if the code is 'broken' then there is a reset button to remove all changes. There are also examples of code that can be altered to change elements such as the size of the 'vehicle' in some games. This combination of a graphical tool and basic coding language can be very useful in the classroom.

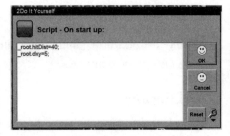

Example of a piece of code for editing (courtesy of Tim Bleazard).

Further ideas can be found on the Ideas to Inspire website (www.ideastoinspire.co.uk).

Interactive worlds

Getting started

The next stage in the programming domain involves tools that combine coding with graphics. The best examples of these are Scratch (http://scratch.mit.edu) and Kodu® (http://bit.ly/downloadkodu). Both are free products that need to be **downloaded** and installed. They build on the concept of 'If … then' statements to control characters and to decide how they work in the environment around them. For example: 'If X happens then move, collect or avoid it.' These can be set to repeat a number of times or even infinitely and elements of scoring can also be incorporated using these tools.

This is how Scratch works:

1. After the software is loaded, users are presented with a main character or sprite. This can be edited, manipulated or removed altogether.
2. Each sprite can be controlled using different commands. These commands are split into blocks such as **Motion**, **Control** or **Sound**.
3. The blocks are combined to perform actions that make the sprite move or respond to other objects.
4. The background can also be painted or edited.

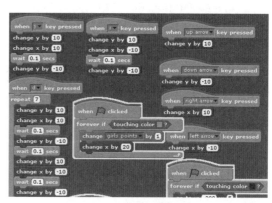
Scratch code

Saved projects can be **uploaded** to the Scratch website, providing the user has a Scratch account. A class account rather than one per child is recommended.

This is how Kodu® works:

1. Once the software is loaded, users can choose whether to load the tutorial or start with a blank screen.
2. Objects are chosen and added to the screen. Each object can have a range of properties, controlled using When and Do statements.
3. Scenery can be manipulated to rise and fall, creating rivers, mountains or bridges.
4. The game can be tested and refined as many times as necessary.

TOP TIP

Kodu® can be controlled using Xbox control pads but this works best if they are wired rather than wireless.

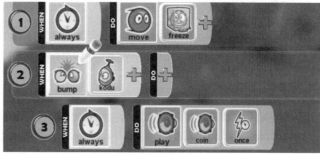
Kodu® code

In the classroom

Cross-curricular

⭐ Animating traditional tales, historical situations, Bible stories, etc. Scratch lends itself to developing simple, scripted animations: the children can take time creating sprites and backgrounds and then write the scripts to have them interact using pre-planned movement and dialogue.

Literacy

⭐ Children could write instructions for either one of their games or for one of the pre-made games within Kodu®.

Maths

⭐ Scratch supports most of the commands used for Logo and Turtle Graphics (simple programming methods) and so lends itself to exploring geometry ideas. Start by drawing squares and triangles and then expand this to more complicated polygons and patterns.

⭐ Scratch can be used to create a simple drill and practice arithmetic game, which could use random numbers to ask questions, e.g. multiplication questions. The game may be made more interesting by using variables to make the questions harder as the score increases.

Modern Foreign Languages

⭐ Interactive conversations. Scratch's Ask, Think and Say coding blocks allow the children to create scripted conversations, either in English or a MFL. A user inputs text and then the Answer variable is used to respond to this input. Recorded audio may then be played back to form a conversation.

Music

⭐ Create an on-screen piano, drum kit or other instrument in Scratch, with each key/drum as its own sprite which then plays an associated sound when clicked.

PE

⭐ Using the 'stadium' template within Kodu®, get the children to design their own game and try this on the field or vice versa. Try to replicate a real game in the Kodu® world.

Science

 20 Questions. Scratch has a block of code that allows If ... Then ... Else ... statements. This code allows simple or more complex branching databases to be constructed, allowing pupils to create their own 20 Questions-style guess the animal games.

 Using the terrain tools in Kodu®, create a new habitat for a creature. Where does it live? What does it eat?

Taking things further

A curriculum guide by the Massachusetts Institute of Technology (the creator of Scratch) is available at http://scratched.media.mit.edu/resources/scratch-curriculum-guide-draft.

Useful tips and resources

Visit the Under Ten Minutes site (www.undertenminutes.com/?p=256) for a brief guide to Scratch.

To set up Kodu®, it is necessary to install other components such as the XNA framework (a Microsoft component needed in order for Kodu® to run). The installation procedure gives prompts to **download** these additions. Videos to help with this process can be found on the Digital Studies Wiki (http://bit.ly/digitalkodu).

More ideas

For those who have tried Scratch and Kodu® and would like to experiment with other aspects of programming and coding, a number of tools are available. These cover two main areas: learning a coding language and applying this language. Although many of these sites and tools tend to be used within secondary schools, some primary-aged children will be able or determined enough to explore them.

Codeacademy – www.codeacademy.com A good starting point to learn a coding language. This is a free site, although a **login** is required to progress beyond the first few stages. In very simple steps, users are shown how to begin programming in JavaScript, a language used throughout the web that provides a basis for children (and teachers) who wish to begin coding. As lessons are completed, users earn badges which they can view on their **online** profile.

Greenfoot www.greenfoot.org A downloadable tool that teaches coding in JavaScript.

KidsRuby – http://kidsruby.com A coding tool that must be downloaded and installed onto a computer. It teaches in a similar way to Codeacademy and is intended for children.

CHAPTER 10 MODELLING AND SIMULATIONS

Introduction

This chapter looks at a range of tools that help to simulate a situation or scenario on the computer. The benefit of such tools is that the scenario can be repeated and the variables changed, often while the simulation is happening; this means that children see the outcomes of their changes in real time.

These tools also allow simulation of scenarios that may prove impossible to create within the classroom.

This chapter covers:

 a range of simulation tools for use within different curriculum areas

 business simulators for enterprise projects designing buildings and 3D models.

It would be possible to plan focused work on using simulations; however, a more practical way of drawing on these tools is to use them when they fit in with other learning that is occurring in the classroom. For example, space simulators should be included when learning about space. Many of the tools mentioned here would not be used for a whole lesson; in fact some take just a few seconds on the whiteboard. Let the children spend some time playing with a range of tools; this does not have to happen during one term but can be spread out across the entire primary phase. The majority of the tools are best used with pairs or groups of children, as this promotes discussion of possible outcomes and strategies for completing the task successfully.

Simple simulations

Getting started

The tools referred to below are generally aimed at Key Stage 2 children unless stated. They are all available on the ICT Planning website (www.ictplanning.co.uk).

1. Once started, the user is provided with some variables to change.
2. The simulation begins and the outcome is displayed.
3. The user can repeat the simulation, deciding whether to keep the variables the same or change them. Sometimes a score is provided to help users judge their performance.

Some children benefit from being shown the simulations first; for others it may be appropriate to let them play first. Although some simulations seem incredibly simple, with teacher input they can lead to valuable discussions.

Simulations in the classroom

Big Day Out – http://bit.ly/bigdayoutsim (Key Stage 1) Has around ten different activities for younger children, including one where they are asked to fit cars onto the Eurostar train. This activity addresses combining numbers to add to ten. The site also has teacher notes to help support the learning.

Create a New Virtual Village – http://bit.ly/villagebuilder Children simply click and create a village; this could then be used as a stimulus for several literacy activities, e.g. designing a setting for a story, writing a postcard from their new village or writing a newspaper article about a new visitor in town.

Duck Builder – http://bit.ly/duckbuilder A downloadable tool that lets children build a duck. They can change the length of its wings and legs, the size of its body and how much it flaps, then wait to see if the duck can fly or if it plummets to the ground. This activity is simple, but it has some potential for storytelling, e.g. why is the duck trying to get away? Where is he going?

Growing Plants – http://bbc.in/bbcplants (Key Stage 1) This tool from the BBC website looks at the effect that water and light can have on a growing plant. The experiment could be repeated a few times removing the water or light and seeing what happens to the plant.

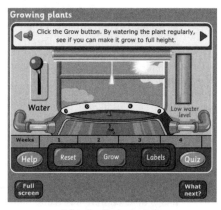
A Growing Plants simulation.

Maths Online – http://bit.ly/mathsonlinesim Has some useful simulators for probability. These include a heads or tails simulator that will toss coins thousands of times. Children can explore to see whether they can match this in the classroom or predict what they think will happen. Is it possible to get ten heads with ten coins? There is also a Dice Simulator (www.dicesimulator.com/) available.

Rabbits and Foxes – http://bit.ly/rabbitfox In this simulator there are three variables: foxes, rabbits and plants. The simulator runs for 50 years and investigates the effects that food chains can have. If there are too many foxes then all of the rabbits will get eaten; if there are too few foxes then the rabbit population will flourish. As the game progresses there is a subtitle to explain what is happening as well as the option to view the information as a graph.

Road Traffic – http://bit.ly/roadtraffic Allows the children to explore traffic. By adjusting the numerous variables, they can experiment to see whether they can keep the traffic moving at a consistent speed. Some of the terms used may need to be explained to the children.

Rollercoaster Creator – http://bit.ly/coaster1 and http://bit.ly/coaster2 – A very simple tool whereby the user adjusts the height of a rollercoaster to get the required score to reach the next level. However, there must be enough gravity and momentum to get the rollercoaster up the hills and down the other sides. This is a useful tool when discussing forces.

Rollercoaster Creator simulation

Sun Aeon Solar System – http://bit.ly/sunaeon This impressive simulator shows the solar system and allows the user to click on a planet to view what happens in the course of an hour, a day, a week or even years. The planets rotate and orbit the sun over time.

Viking Quest – http://bbc.in/vikingquest This game casts the player as a Viking leader. Choices to make include where to set up camp, what type of people to have in your crew and which route to take. As children progress through the screens they are shown how Viking boats are made and presented with other interesting Viking facts.

Taking things further

There is a range of simulation-based puzzles on the Caret Brain Teaser site (http://puzzling.caret.cam.ac.uk/index.php). Although the majority of them are aimed at secondary school children, some would work well with primary children too.

You're fired!

Getting started

Although the majority of tools mentioned within this book can be used in different ways across a range of topics, the tools listed in this section are generally applicable to one specific topic area. However, this is an area that increasing numbers of schools are now including within their curriculum; sometimes known as an 'enterprise' topic, it generally involves either running a business or creating a product to share/sell to others. The topic can be based on a number of ideas, from *Dragons' Den* to *The Apprentice* and offers a very rich and varied learning experience for children. Although not specifically ICT based, there are a number of ways in which ICT can enhance the enterprise topic.

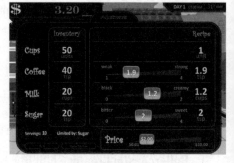

The options in the Coffee Shop Game.

When it comes to enterprise, it is helpful if the children have some prior experience of running a mini-business. This is where simulation tools are so valuable. There are two main tools that assist children with their businesses: the Lemonade Game (www.coolmath-games.com/lemonade/) and the Coffee Shop Game (www.coolmath-games.com/0-coffee-shop/index.html).

This is how these websites work:

1. The players purchases a range of ingredients.
2. They then choose the quality and quantity of ingredients.
3. The game simulates a day's business and a daily total is calculated.
4. If there is enough money left, the business can run for another day.
5. Along the way there are variables to consider, e.g. ice will only last a day or milk will go off.
6. Children are given a final score, or bank balance, at the end of the simulation.

These are fairly simple activities, but the sites offer numerous challenges to extend the tasks into the future. For example:

Is it possible to run the business for 14 days without going bankrupt?

What is the highest profit that can be made in the time given?

What factors need to to be considered when selling their product? (weather, price)

Does customer satisfaction matter?

In both games, the more stock that is purchased, the cheaper it becomes per unit. So the children must work out how much they should charge depending on the cost of their ingredients and materials. Charging customers less than this will result in a loss, but since some ingredients spoil at the end of the day anyway, keeping them is not worthwhile.

In the classroom

Before a 'real' business is launched, there are numerous ways in which the two games can be incorporated across the curriculum.

Design technology

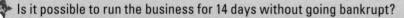 The ice in the lemonade game melts each day. Design packaging to keep it cold.

ICT

 Collect the data on a spreadsheet and use the functions to help with more complicated sums throughout the week.

Literacy

 Write instructions for creating the perfect coffee or jug of lemonade.

Maths

 Ask the children to note down their profit or loss each day and make a graph to represent their results. This could be extended to consider trends: does the graph show consistent profit or were there days when the business struggled? Why was this?

 Encourage the children to work out the percentage they will make on, for example, each cup of drink. If the ingredients cost £1 per cup and they sell each cup for £2.50, what percentage profit is this?

 What is the most the business could make per day? The Coffee Shop Game indicates how many cups can be made; if all of these are sold, what would be the takings for that day?

Science

 The games rely on the principle of supply and demand so encourage children to explore factors which may affect this.

 The temperature on each day is shown. What is this in Celsius? Does the temperature of the day affect what we would want to drink? Would we need warm drinks on a cold day or cold drinks on a hot day?

Taking things further

When children have attempted to run virtual businesses, the next logical step is to try and replicate this process with a real business.

After introducing the task, and possibly showing suitable clips from *The Apprentice*, ask the children to write persuasive letters to the head teacher asking for funds to start their business. The letter should explain why the funds are needed and what they are going to be used for. Check with the head teacher to ensure permission for the project, and that funds are available.

When funds are secured, the children can start to think about the details of their project. Divide the class into small groups of three or four, and discuss possible business ideas. These could include: selling cakes/drinks; putting on a talent show and charging the audience an entry fee; art and craft activities such as making photo frames with a sprayed-gold pasta border; or competitions with an entry fee, such as a penalty shootout competition.

After choosing the business, the children can start to research the setting-up costs. What ingredients or stock will they need to purchase? Will they need to make anything before the business is ready? What is their potential profit? Children may need to check the websites of a number of different online shops to compare the cost of their products before purchasing them.

Aspects to consider:

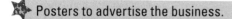 Posters to advertise the business.

Spreadsheets to keep track of costs and profits.

Creating a risk assessment if necessary.

Money work – ensure the children are confident handling money and giving change.

When the businesses have been running for a few days, hold group/class discussions about profits and where they will go.

This kind of project motivates children and relates to several areas of the curriculum.

Become an architect

Getting started

SketchUp (http://sketchup.google.com) is a tool for creating graphical representations of buildings and other monuments. It has huge potential, yet is also simple enough that children will enjoy creating basic shapes and buildings.

This is how SketchUp works:

1. Children begin by drawing simple 2D shapes.
2. These can be extended to make them 3D.
3. They can be combined with other shapes to create buildings.
4. Textures and paint effects can be added to the creations.

The site also offers the 3D warehouse (http://sketchup.google.com/3dwarehouse): an online gallery of creations made by other users.

To make a simple house design, follow these steps:

Use the rectangle tool to draw the base of the house.	
Use the push/pull tool to change the rectangle into a cuboid.	
Draw a line along the top part of the rectangle as close to the middle as possible.	
Use the move tool to drag this line up to make a pointed roof.	
Use different shapes to add doors, windows, etc.	
Use the paint bucket to decorate the house.	

In the classroom

Usually two or three lessons are adequate to familiarise children with the basics of SketchUp.

Art

 Use the different models to create a 3D piece of artwork.

Design technology

 Used SketchUp as a tool to model a design before creating it for real.

History

 Can children replicate the Great Pyramids of Egypt? Or rebuild London after the Great Fire?

Literacy

 Write instructions for creating a simple house or building.

Maths

 Use SketchUp to explore 3D models and/or use the measuring tool to work out the area and volume of shapes.

Science

 Look at different habitats and design a new habitat for a creature or a house for someone living in a warm or cold climate. Explain the different features that have been included.

Whole school

 Design a new school, considering the layout and features to include.

> **TOP TIP**
>
> Under Ten Minutes (www.undertenminutes.com) has a how-to guide for SketchUp.

Taking things further

Combining SketchUp with Augmented Reality is the AR-media tool (http://bit.ly/sketchupar) which provides an image of the building created on SketchUp then effectively places it on the desk in front of the child. The free version of this **software** works well and is impressive.

The Lego Digital Designer (http://ldd.lego.com/) allows children to create virtual Lego™ models on their computer. The tool needs to be downloaded and finished models can be **uploaded** onto the online gallery.

CHAPTER 11 SOCIAL MEDIA

Blogs for children

The section on blogging will consider two distinct areas; the use of blogging by, with and for children to share learning, and the CPD (continuing professional development) aspect of blogging used in training and for sharing teaching practice.

More and more schools are using blogging as a quick and easy way of sharing children's work with an audience. This was traditionally achieved by printing children's work and sharing it on walls within the school or possibly on the school website, but blogging takes this a bit further. A common problem with school websites is that, even with an area on which to share children's work, access is limited to a few members of staff. With blogging it is possible to provide accounts for a range of users, each with differing levels of access. For example, children may be able to write on the **blog** but cannot post it before a teacher checks the content of the post.

What is a blog?

The name 'blog' stems from 'web-log' and describes a website that is often used for news items and allows users to write a post that appears at the top of the page. Posts are generally displayed chronologically. Visitors to the posts can leave comments, ranging from children admiring each others' work to parents expressing pride in their child. Blog posts can contain text, images or embedded content such as Animoto slideshows, or Google Maps (see Chapter 6). Blogs can often have a number of **widgets** and plugin that help them to do more, such as tracking where visitors to the blog come from. This is useful when working with children as they enjoy seeing the world map fill with markers to show how far their work has reached. A list of useful widgets can be found at http://stjohnsblogs.co.uk/which-plugins/.

A map of visitors.

When starting to blog, think about the immediate audience you are trying to reach — this will often be other classes within your school and parents. Visitors to your blog from other countries are a bonus!

It can be difficult for you to fit blogging into a busy timetable; one method is setting aside time each week to blog one aspect of the children's learning. To begin with, this may be once a week but, as you (and children) become more engaged, blogging may become more frequent as different opportunities arise. The easiest way to start writing posts is to talk about what has been happening in class. As part of a plenary session at the end of a lesson or at the end of a day, discuss with the children what they have been doing that they would like to share with their parents. An effective approach is to take suggestions from children and type their ideas. As the blog post is written (it only needs to be a few sentences), the children can suggest ways to improve it; this then takes the form of a useful group-writing session. Promote the blog using traditional methods, such as the school newsletter, or make a link to it on the school website.

As confidence develops, you may wish to add photos and videos to the blog. This is simple to do with most blogging platforms. Encourage the children to take ownership and write posts too. Begin this by logging in for them and letting a pair of children write the blog post as part of a writing activity. At the end of the lesson, discuss as a class what was written, how it could be improved and check for errors. As the children become more familiar with blogging, they can be given their own usernames. It is free to start a blog, but there are a number of things to consider when doing so.

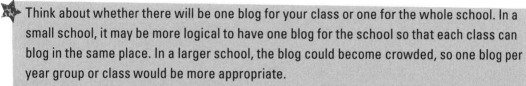

Think about whether there will be one blog for your class or one for the whole school. In a small school, it may be more logical to have one blog for the school so that each class can blog in the same place. In a larger school, the blog could become crowded, so one blog per year group or class would be more appropriate.

Think about which platform to use. Many platforms have broadly similar features but there are differences in terms of the features provided. Although it is free to start blogging, schools may find that they require additional features and are therefore prepared to pay for their blogs. Generally, free blogs have a limited amount of storage space.

Blogging platforms

WordPress.com – www.wordpress.com Takes just a few minutes to get started and is completely free. It offers around 80 templates to begin with. Your blog address would be something like class6.wordpress.com although it is possible to purchase an address such as www.class6blog.com. A how-to video can be found at www.undertenminutes.com/?p=56.

Primary Blogger – www.primaryblogger.co.uk Uses the WordPress blogs, but includes a range of themes and plugins to benefit schools. WordPress is used by bloggers across the world, whereas the Primary Blogger team has thought about the best approach for use in schools.

'Self-hosted' WordPress – www.wordpress.org For users who want a greater level of control over the WordPress site. Download the WordPress **software** from the site and install it on the webspace owned by the school or an external company. Schools can then install a range of themes and plugins to suit their needs. Purchasing an address or domain name and some web storage is fairly inexpensive.

Posterous – www.posterous.com, **Typepad** – www.typepad.com or **Blogger** – www.blogger.com Posterous and Typepad are two blogging platforms commonly used in schools. Posterous is extremely quick to use but provides minimal options for changing the theme and look of the site. Typepad allows users to create a website and blogging platform in one. Blogger, not to be confused with Primary Blogger, is Google's blogging platform. It works in a similar way to the other blogging tools listed here. Examples include http://weedonbec.posterous.com/ and www.porchester.notts.sch.uk/.

Many of the features of blogs are available in Learning Platforms too; however there are two main differences. Firstly, the Learning Platform usually costs significantly more per year than a blog does; secondly, the Learning Platform tends to be private and hidden away. Although this is extremely safe, comments and feedback will be limited. Children gain a lot from sharing their learning publicly and in a few steps (see below) a blog can become as safe as a Learning Platform.

E-safety

Although visitors to a blog can leave comments, it is prudent to ensure they leave an email address to verify their identity. This also helps to reduce spam comments. Check the settings for the blog to ensure that comments require approval before going live. This gives you an additional layer of protection to prevent inappropriate comments appearing on the blog.

With tools such as WordPress, it is also possible to create additional users with limited functionality. For example, children could be given the ability to post new items but not to publish them for public viewing before having them checked.

Leave a Reply

Your email address will not be published.

Name

Mr Addison

Email

Website

Comment

You may use these HTML tags and attributes: <a href="" title=""> <abbr title=""> <acronym title=""> <b> <blockquote cite=""> <cite> <code> <del datetime=""> <em> <i> <q cite=""> <strike> <strong>

Post Comment

A comment box

In the classroom

The key idea of a blog is to share learning and experiences with an audience, but there are other ways in which a blog can be used within the class.

1. Use the blog to write a story. Share ideas as a class and write on the blog each day to create a complete story across a unit of work.
2. For a homework session, ask the children to read the blog post and leave a comment as a reply.
3. Posts can be written at any time and set to go live on the site at a particular time; these timed posts can be used to good effect. Claire Lotriet shares an experience she tried with her class:

'We wrote a blog post that we set to go live in the morning before the children went to school. They had been asked to check it at 8am and the post asked the children to pick five things that they would take with them if they were escaping their house and becoming a refugee. When the children came to school we then discussed their objects and they took part in a refugee day, learning what refugees were and thinking more about the plight of refugees around the world.'

One of the major tools for promoting writing and blogging has been the 100 Word Challenge (www.100wc. net). This is a weekly prompt set by Julia Skinner, a retired head teacher. The prompt is either a few words or a picture and children are encouraged to write a piece of text that is 100 words long. This is put onto their blog and linked on the 100 Word Challenge site. Julia (and her team of helpers) then leave comments for the children and choose some to highlight each week.

Many schools use the 100 Word Challenge as an activity for children within class and sometimes this forms part of the literacy lesson. Simon McLoughin went further and wrote about a lesson where he linked with another school to take part in the challenge together (http://bit.ly/HMppAl).

Reaching a wider audience

One of the potential stumbling blocks to starting a blog is the lack of an audience to read the posts. Reaching a worldwide audience is not necessarily the first thing to consider when blogging, but it does help to enthuse the children.

Some teachers have started projects with the specific aim of providing teachers and classes with an audience. The most successful of these is Quad Blogging (www.quadblogging.net). Each term classes are put into groups of four and each week one of their blogs becomes the focus. During this focused week, other classes leave comments on any blog posts. Over the term, each class blog has a chance to be the focus. A smaller project is Blog Adopt (www.blogadopt.net) which uses a similar scheme but with pairs of classes rather than groups.

Blogs for teachers

Teachers use blogging for two main reasons: to read other blogs to find ideas, resources and inspiration, and to actually write a blog to share ideas or reflect on their practice.

The Twitter section below lists several blogs. To read these, viewers can either go directly to the address to check it sporadically or use a tool to manage this blog reading more efficiently. One example is Google Reader (www.google.com/reader) – this requires a Google Account in order to sign up.

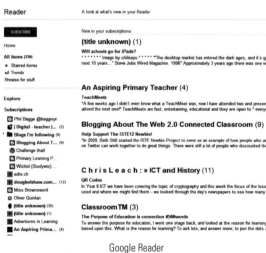

Google Reader

After signing in, blogs can be copied and pasted into the reader. The blogs are then listed, along with any unread items. Users have the option to view the blog in its own site rather than in the reader and there is also an **app** to read blogs on mobile phones.

Example blogs include:

 Rising Stars – www.risingstars-uk.com/blog/   2Simple – www.2simpletalk.com/

 Microsoft Education – http://blogs.msdn.com/b/teachers/

However they are read, blogs are a valuable way of keeping up with other teachers or organisations, and finding out about new developments and thoughts. More and more teachers are starting to blog simply to describe what is happening within their class (e.g. to share a new tool). The number of blogs by teachers is now such that the range of topics and issues covered is extensive; rather than worrying that a blog post has been missed, it is advisable merely to dip in and out of a blog or selection of blogs – this alone will be beneficial.

Writing a blog

Guidance for writing a blog as a teacher is similar to the guidance for blogging with children. The same tools can be used and, as mentioned previously, it is useful to start with a free tool before deciding whether to pay for hosting and a more personal domain name.

Consider the layout of the blog and which additional features you wish to include, such as links to Twitter accounts or a visitor map. It is crucial that posts should remain professional at all times. A key message to remember, and to share with the children, is that anyone could look at the blog.

A plugin or service such as Twitterfeed (http://twitterfeed.com) enables the blog posts to be automatically posted onto Twitter, which can help to increase the audience. However, many teachers start blogging without the desire for an audience. A blog provides a platform on which to reflect on life as a teacher, and the associated experiences and emotions.

Twitter

Increasing numbers of teachers are using Twitter to meet like-minded people, find out new ideas to share their learning. Although there are **networks** for sharing ideas on sites such as Facebook or Google+, Twitter seems to be the most popular. The majority of readers of this book will fall into one of three categories:

1. You are already a Twitter user and know how well it can be used to support your teaching career; in fact that might be how you found this book in the first place.
2. You are on Twitter but use it for other reasons or purposes.
3. You are not on Twitter and it sounds like a source of celebrity gossip rather than a way of sharing ideas.

What is Twitter?

Twitter is best explained using analogies. The first is to think of Twitter as a newsagent or bookshop containing stories and information from a range of sources; some of these are linked to your chosen career, some to hobbies and interests, and some will be of no use what-so-ever. If a teacher on Twitter follows other teachers they can share ideas; if they follow celebrities they will get celebrity gossip.

Key terminology

A tweet.

Direct Message – This is a private message sent between two people who follow each other.

Favourites – Tweets can be 'favourited' to look through later. It can be difficult to search through.

Followers/Following – Users on Twitter have followers. This is not the same as friends on Facebook, for example, as it does not need to be a mutual agreement. Person A can follow person B without B following him/her back.

Hashtag – This is a keyword linked to a subject. If users search for this word, they will find all the related tweets. Some educational examples include #ictcurric or #ukedchat. For more, see below.

PLN (Personal Learning Network) – Due to the fact that everyone on Twitter follows different people, some have commented that this is like having a personal learning network to share ideas with.

Protected tweets – To follow others, users can simply press the 'follow' button, but if users are protected they need to approve followers first. The users receive an email saying someone would like to follow them.

Retweet – A message that has been shared by someone who wasn't the original author. If one person writes the original tweet, people following this can then retweet (share) this with their followers.

Tweet – A message posted on Twitter; limited to 140 characters it is a short update that can be text, a link or picture.

Username – This starts with the '@' symbol. For example, @ianaddison or @ohlottie.

The first 24 hours

To register an account, visit www.twitter.com and sign up. Choose a username and follow the steps.

When starting on Twitter, think about are your profile and your picture. The picture does not necessarily need to be personal, but leaving it at the default may reduce the likelihood of others following the account. It is also useful to write a brief biography on the profile to explain your role and location. This does not need to be too specific, but again it helps others to decide whether to follow your account or not. The profile should state that you are a teacher as this will help other teachers who check it.

A list of suggestions is provided below for accounts that you may wish to follow (around 10 to 20 is probably a good starting point). It is also possible to see who they are following and then follow some of those accounts too. You can let people know that you are following them by saying hello.

Where to start?

Some of the people below have helped to write sections of this book; all have helped to inspire teachers.

@**bevevans22** – Bev is a teacher from Wales who specialises in learning with young children and those with special needs. She is also the expert behind the Autoshape **clipart** ideas. http://technostories. wordpress.com/

@**chrisleach78** – Chris is an ICT leader at an independent school in Northamptonshire. He is also behind the Rethinking ICT website (http://rethinkingict.wordpress.com/). http://chrisleach78.wordpress.com/

@**daviderogers** – David is a multi-award winning secondary geography teacher in Hampshire and part of the Geography Collective. http://daviderogers.blogspot.co.uk/

@**dawnhallybone** – Dawn is a teacher from London who has won awards for her pioneering work with games-based learning in the classroom. http://hallyd.edublogs.org/

@**ideas_factory** – Julian is a deputy head teacher and won a Microsoft Innovative Educator award for his work with QR codes (see Chapter 12) to improve learning. http://ideasfactory.me

@**kvnmcl** – Kevin is a teacher and is extremely passionate about personalising learning for children. He has written a great deal about adapting his planning and classroom to enhance learning. www.ictsteps.com

@**markw29** – Mark created Ideas to Inspire as well as several other websites such as Teaching Ideas. www.teachingideas.co.uk

@**mberry** – Miles is the ICT leader at the University of Roehampton and also chair of NAACE (National Association for Able Children in Education) http://milesberry.net/

@**ohlottie** – Claire is a Year 6 teacher and ICT coordinator in Croydon. www.clairelotriet.com

@**primarypete** – Pete is an advanced skills teacher who teaches in Key Stage 1 and has blogged about his use of Playbooks as well as being a keen Zondle user. www.primarypete.net

@**simcloughlin** – Simon is a Year 5 teacher in the north of England and uses his blog to share a variety of ideas. http://simcloughlin.com/

@simonhaughton – Simon is the creator of numerous websites, including the Infant Encyclopedia. www.simonhaughton.co.uk/

@tombarrett – Tom is the teacher behind the Maths Maps and also started the Interesting Ways series. www.edte.ch/blog

@timrylands – Tim is an inspirational speaker who works with teachers and children across the world. He is well known for his use of games to help writing. www.timrylands.com/

The first week

Quite quickly, most users find that the Twitter website is not ideal for following conversations and move towards software or apps that can manage Twitter instead, such as TweetDeck (www.tweetdeck.com) or HootSuite (www.hootsuite.com). Indeed, new users may find it easier to find a good app for Twitter on their phone or tablet rather than the website.

TOP TIP

An interesting post on the usefulness of Twitter can be found on Mark Anderson's blog http://ictevangelist.com/?p=805.

It is important to try and share some thoughts with the world as well as listening to what others have to say. It does not matter if you repeat something that has been said before; someone somewhere may be inspired by the ideas that you share.

Into the future

As users become more familiar with Twitter, some find that they want to check constantly for new messages. However it does not matter if there is not enough time to check Twitter every hour of every day. Use it rather as an additional resource and a way of connecting with other teachers to share ideas and links.

Some useful hashtags

The following hashtags are used regularly in education:

- **#dlchat** – Talks about Digital Leaders, the groups of children in school that are given extra responsibility.

- **#ictcurric** – A secondary-based tag that looks at ways of improving the ICT curriculum, but there are often ideas that are applicable to primary school as well.

- **#ukedchat** – Follows on from an American tag, #edchat, a weekly discussion about an educational topic. The #ukedchat conversation is held every Thursday between 8–9pm but tweets appear throughout the week with an educational focus.

CHAPTER 12 OTHER USEFUL TOOLS

Sharing links

Getting started

With such a wide variety of websites and **online** tools being shared with children, it is important to make sure they can access them without difficulty. Some tools are easily found via search engines but for children, especially younger ones, clicking a link to a website is the most straightforward option. This reduces the potential for errors when typing addresses into a **browser**, and also reduces the amount of time to load the site in the first place. A further benefit of sharing links online is that children can access the sites at home.

The first place to share links should be on the school website or blog. Links must be easy to find and also easy to access. There are various tools that enable you to link to a particular site from the school website. Teachers only need to set up the main page once, and can then edit the links page as often as necessary.

3x3 Links – www.3x3links.com Requires a Google **login**. Once signed in, users see a grid of nine squares. Each of these squares can be used to hold a link or a folder. Within a folder the squares can then hold links or yet more folders. Although probably too many for children, it is possible to have hundreds of links in total. This feature could be used across the school with each class or year group being given their own square to add links to.

Using the options **menus**, it is possible to add a vanity **URL** which provides a shorter, more personal address for children to access such as www.3x3links.com/stjohn.

An example page can be found at http://bit.ly/stjohnslinks.

St John's 3 x 3 Links page.

Satpin – www.satpin.com This site does not require a login, meaning websites can be grouped together in seconds. Simply visit the site, choose a background and then add links. Change the main title of the page and then click the 'lock' icon in the top-right corner of the screen. There the URL is displayed; this is the page that is then shared with children.

An example page, showing four links, is available at http://satpin.com/red4122.

Avatars

Getting started

A range of free tools provide children with the opportunity to create new characters (or **avatars**) that can be used in place of a child's photograph. This character could be used on a blog or website for children who are not permitted to use their photograph.

This is how these websites work:

1. Children choose from a range of character features such as eyes and hair.
2. Props are added.   3. The picture is saved or **downloaded**.

> **TOP TIP** ✓
>
> Some sites do not allow the resulting picture to be downloaded; in these cases, take a screenshot instead.

In the classroom

Art

 Produce a collage showing the children as avatars.

Cross-curricular

 Create a class display with a difference: a class 'photo' of everyone's avatar.

Design technology

 Create a vehicle or base for your superhero avatar.

ICT

 Create a class photo slideshow of the different avatars that have been created, for example http://stjohnsblogs.co.uk/class5/build-your-wildself/.

Literacy

 Use the avatar tools to create characters for a story.

Create a superhero and then use this character as the star of a story or news report. How did the superhero save the day?

Maths

 When everyone has created an avatar, use graphing tools to compare and contrast them. How many have brown hair? Blue eyes? Wings?

Music

 Create a superhero and compose a theme tune for him/her.

Science

 Use the Build Your Wild Self tool (www.buildyourwildself.com) to create a new kind of creature. Discuss what this creature may eat and where it might live. Link this to work on habitats and adaptation by discussing why the creature would be suited to a habitat.

 Think about food chains and discuss what sort of creature would be above or below the Build Your Wild Self creature.

Useful tips and resources

The primary school ICT avatar tool (http://primaryschoolict.com/avatars/) lists some avatar creation tools suitable for use within the classroom.

Talking characters

Getting started

The most recognised site for creating talking characters is Voki (www.voki.com). This has a range of characters to choose from that may be given voices. They can also speak different languages, although there is no translate feature so, if children are unable to type in the target language, it might be worth checking with an online translating tool first.

This is how Voki works:

A Voki character.

1. Choose a character from the selection or use the die to find a random character.
2. Decorate the character using hats, jewellery and other assorted props.
3. Type some text for the character to read.
4. Adjust the voice if necessary.
5. Save and then embed the character onto a **blog**.

There is a range of options for adjusting the voice but many are not particularly useful.

In the classroom

Voki characters can be used online in any context requiring an instruction or speaking part, e.g. introducing visitors to your blog or website. On a blog, the Voki could set a task for the children. One school used a wizard Voki to set science challenges for children.

History

 Create a Voki for a historical figure and use the text box to include a speech he/she might have made.

Literacy

 Try to design a Voki to match a character within a story. What does he/she sound like? What would he/she say?

Modern foreign languages

 As Voki speak different languages, this enables the children to listen to instructions given in the target foreign language before translating them or working out a reply.

Useful tips and resources

An educational version of Voki, for a small fee, provides usernames for a number of children. The usernames can be a little complex, but teachers do have the option to set 'lessons' and tasks for children so that when they login they create a Voki for a specific purpose.

A similar tool is Zimmer Twins (http://zimmertwinsatschool.com). Although this is slightly more like an animated movie, it still offers the opportunity to share instructions or information with children.

Note-taking

Getting started

Collaborative notes first became popular with the use of a site called Wallwisher (www.wallwisher.com) but there are now a number of other sites that work in a similar way. Some of these do require a login. Each of these sites starts with a blank wall or board onto which users can add notes or items.

This is how these websites work:

1. Someone creates a blank page or board with a unique URL.
2. This URL is shared with children.
3. The children add notes to the page, usually by double-clicking.
4. Each note can contain text or a link, and sometimes pictures or videos can also be added.

In the classroom

These note-taking tools provide a great way of collaborating ideas and questions. They can usually be embedded into a blog, meaning that children's notes are available at home or that the children can be set the task of populating the board as homework. It is useful to have an online question board available throughout a topic so children can continually add their questions and ideas. This would also work well with an analogue board, created using paper-based sticky notes. The tools can also be used to collect ideas of what the children already know about a topic as well as what they would like to find out.

Art

- Collect images to showcase examples of art that demonstrate good use of a particular artistic element, e.g. tone or colour.
- Share examples of children's artwork or those of a famous artist to make a class gallery.

Cross-curricular

- Evaluate a lesson or topic by asking the children to share their thoughts and opinions.
- After the children have created online work, e.g. pictures or their own websites, use the notes board to collect examples.
- Use the board as a target wall: what are the children's targets for the week or term? Are these targets being met?

Literacy

- Encourage the children to add examples of adverbs, similes and sentence starters to the notes, to generate a useful class collection.
- Write words and sentences to describe a picture, character or setting.
- Use the notes board to list reasons for and against, as part of a discussion or debate.

Maths

- Ask the children to search for 'mathematical' images when they are out and about and to include these on their board, e.g. 'Buy 2 for £3' offers. They could then calculate how much money each offer would save them.
- Search for images of shapes online and add these to create a range of pictures to explore.
- Create a board for a number, e.g. 27. Each note shows a different way of reaching the target number, e.g. 3 x 9 or 30 − 3.

Useful tips and resources

Corkboard.me – www.corkboard.me The free version of Corkboard provides very few functions, just the option to click and add a note. However, this makes it extremely simple for use within the classroom. If users do wish to add images, they can paste a URL into the note to create a link. If this is the URL of an image, it will display the picture instead of the address.

Lino – http://en.linoit.com/ Sticky notes are dragged onto the board rather than double-clicked. Stickies can be set to 'private' and may also have due dates assigned to them making this a useful tool for a to-do list or project.

PrimaryWall – http://primarywall.com/ Does not require a login and sticky notes can be added in seconds. When creating a wall, the URL is often very random. To remedy this, instead of clicking 'create wall', type a word or phrase after the address such as http://primarywall.com/ictessentials. Providing no one has used this word/phrase before, this address becomes yours. It is also possible to automatically sort the notes to make reading much easier and clearer.

PrimaryWall (courtesy of John McLear)

Wallwisher – www.wallwisher.com When creating a board, users are given the choice of a web address. Wallwisher provides a short amount of space for text and another box for a link to a website or picture. This makes collecting images very quick and ensures it does not take long to build a class gallery.

TOP TIP

It is useful to check the visibility of a wall before using it with children, as some sites make the wall private so that only the creator can see it. Sometimes there is also the option for a teacher to check the notes before they appear live on the page.

QR codes

What are they?

This is a QR code or quick response code.

A QR code is a matrix code created by the Japanese corporation Denso-Wave, a subsidiary of Toyota, in 1994. They created QR codes to track car parts.

Simply put, a QR code is a 3D barcode, but a more sophisticated version of the barcode is printed, for example, on a carton of milk.

You use an **app** on a mobile device to 'scan' a QR code; it can then link to a video,

A QR code to Rising Stars.

contact details (e.g. an email address or phone number) or a website.

To 'scan' a QR code, the following are necessary:

- A device that has a camera to scan or take a picture of the code.

- A program to do the decoding.

- Web access to see where the code takes you.

This limits you to mobile devices or the new iPod Touch.

In most cases QR codes are used as a marketing strategy for businesses and they usually appear on signs, packaging and other advertisements. B & Q has used them to link to videos on 'How to put up wallpaper' and Pepsi used them to provide access to an exclusive competition.

QR codes are free to produce and scan. In addition, the colour can be customised and images added.

So how can a marketing tool work for teachers?

A QR code generator.

Getting started

Creating a QR code

1. Most QR code generators are online; use a simple one such as Delivr (www.delivr.com/qr-code-generator) or MyQR (www.myqr.co).
2. Select the Text option and write a message in the box provided.
3. Press 'Generate QR Code'.
4. This will create a QR code that can be saved to your computer as an image and printed out.

After using these websites to practise generating QR codes, **download** a QR code reader for your mobile device so that you can view what is 'stored' on the QR code. These are available in the 'app-store' of your mobile device or you can search on the **internet**. Some reliable QR code mobile-device apps are Qrafter, Optiscan, i-nigma and QuickMark.

I have an app but how do I 'scan' the QR codes?

To scan QR codes, start the QR scanner app on your mobile device and follow the on-screen instructions. You may see a frame in which to focus the QR code. Align the QR code in this box, and the application will scan and read the QR code data. You may have to click or tap the web address to continue to the site.

What other things can a QR code represent?

As QR codes have become more sophisticated, the list of things they can be generated for has grown. Currently, you can produce a QR code for the following:

- Twitter, Facebook, LinkedIn and Foursquare messages: scan a QR code and it will send a message on your social media account.

- Text/email message: a QR code that auto-sends a text/email message.

- Contact details: when scanned it shows a list of contact details such as email, phone number, address, etc.

- Online videos such as Youtube: scan a code to link to a video.

- Google Maps: set a QR code to be linked to any place on a Google Map.

- A calendar event: create a code that automatically puts an event into your phone calendar.

- iTunes link, PayPal 'Buy it now' and **Skype** calls.

In the classroom

Cross-curricular

- Add QR codes to Word documents for the children to check their answers.

- Add QR codes to classroom displays to make them interactive.

Geography

- Make a QR-code guided tour: during a fieldtrip, give the children multiple QR codes that provide additional information about different locations on the trip.

- The QR Treasure Hunt Generator (www.classtools.net/QR/) is easy to use, free and creates a series of QR codes for you to use in a treasure hunt. Codes are created for questions and answers.

Literacy

- Ask the children to write children's books and then record them reading their work. **Upload** the audio online and add a QR code linking to the audio for each page of the book to create an interactive reading experience.

- Do you have an inspirational quote or classic poem displayed in your classroom? Use a QR code that brings up a photograph of the author or links to a podcast of the poem.

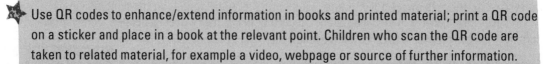

➤ Use QR codes to enhance/extend information in books and printed material; print a QR code on a sticker and place in a book at the relevant point. Children who scan the QR code are taken to related material, for example a video, webpage or source of further information.

➤ Create a 'choose your own adventure' story featuring individual QR codes that need to be scanned in order to advance through the story.

Maths

➤ Provide children with data on a paper handout plus a QR code for an online graphing tool such as Create a Graph (www.idsfac.me/cr8agraph).

➤ Create a maths worksheet that has a QR code beside each problem. Upon scanning the code a step-by-step tutorial is launched in YouTube explaining the process of solving the problem. Children can use these when struggling with a particular problem or to check their result.

➤ When learning about money, many children set up 'class shops'. Add another dimension to this by pricing some of the class shop items with QR codes. Children can scan these to find out the price in the same way that items would have their barcodes scanned at the checkout of a real shop. After some time, have a '10%-off everything sale' and give children the responsibility of adjusting the prices linked to the QR codes.

Music

➤ Create QR codes that link to podcasts of classical music. When playing the music in class, attach the related code to the particular piece of music itself, so children can listen to the recording at home.

Science

➤ Attach QR codes to a physical object to allow for a thorough exploration of the object, e.g. to a skeleton, with links to multimedia providing further information.

Whole school

➤ Print QR codes that point to your classroom homework/events calendar. Ask the children to attach them to their agendas or daily planners.

➤ Create a virtual tour of the school and give visitors/inspectors a device when they arrive.

Put some QR codes around the school, e.g. one in the entrance (linking to the school mission statement or address of school website), one in the corridor (linking to the school vision) and so on.

Taking things further: customisation

Standard QR codes are black and white, but a number of online custom-QR-code generators allow you to change the colour, add images, round the edges and tilt the angle of the code. Three useful, free sites are: QR Hacker (www.qrhacker.com), QR Stuff (www.qrstuff.com) and Unitag (www.unitaglive.com).

A customised QR code (courtesy Julian Wood).

Useful tips and resources

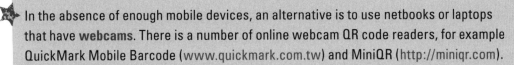

When generating QR codes simply to display text, an internet connection is not needed in order to read the text. This can be useful for clue-based treasure hunts around places with no Wi-Fi connection.

In the absence of enough mobile devices, an alternative is to use netbooks or laptops that have **webcams**. There is a number of online webcam QR code readers, for example QuickMark Mobile Barcode (www.quickmark.com.tw) and MiniQR (http://miniqr.com).

To investigate QR codes in more depth, a list of 'QR codes in Education' **weblinks** can be found at www.idsfac.me/QRinEdu.

Geocaching

What is geocaching?

Geocaching is a global treasure hunting activity that uses GPS (Global Positioning Systems) to help find small containers or caches. GPS is the same technology that helps a car's satellite navigation system work and it essentially pinpoints your position on the Earth's surface using satellites. The main feature of geocaching is that it is an outdoor activity, allowing core curriculum goals to be met while engaging children in tasks outside of the classroom environment.

There are millions of geocaches set up around the world that can be used to explore the different areas. It is also relatively simple to set up your own basic caches around the school grounds and even possible to set up and design caches for people the other side of the world to find.

Some basic, inexpensive equipment is needed (see below), and it is entirely possible to run effective sessions with a small number of handheld GPS devices.

Getting started

A handheld device that has a GPS function is required for geocaching. The Garmin eTrex is robust and reliable for use in schools. It is easy to use as you simply enter the coordinates into the device.

The proliferation of smartphones also allows easy access to geocaching apps. There is a range of supported platforms, including Windows phones, the iPhone, iPod Touch and Android devices (www. geocaching.com/live/default.aspx). These apps allow you to access the geocaching website and locate caches easily.

Many schools are using geocaching activities successfully with one class set of five or six devices – this also encourages collaboration and develops teamwork skills.

There are two ways in which to use geocaching. The simplest is to log on to www.geocaching.com and find caches in your local area. Program in their location and head out to find them. The second way enables you to hide caches around your school. Using a GPS handheld device you can share their location with the class, and then set children the task of finding them.

 Before starting a geocaching activity, children need to understand the coordinate system of longitude and latitude. It is also helpful to talk about satellites and conduct some simple research into how GPS works.

 Children will need some basic training in how to use the handheld devices, in particular how to enter the coordinates of the cache they wish to find and how to use the 'Go-to' feature.

In the classroom

The main purpose of geocaching is to get out of the classroom. This often increases motivation and engagement in children. Many of the following ideas provide a good introduction to geocaching for children, and several can be extended to encompass other curriculum areas and further children's learning.

Art

 Geocaching is a secret activity and, as such, geocaches should blend into their environment. Indeed, geocaching experts refer to those who don't know about geocaches as 'Muggles'. With the children, explore the school grounds or a local fieldwork site and take photographs of the area. Collect samples of material such as leaves, twigs and stones. Back in the classroom, describe the area in writing or through sketches and drawings. When the class understands their area, they can design a secret, camouflaged cache that will be difficult to see with the naked eye. Children can then build their cache and hide it in location. In doing so, they could use the materials gathered. Ask the children to write a hint so that others can find their hidden treasure! Incorporate this idea within a unit about habitats or the local environment.

 Extend the activity above into a larger-scale project. Vote or hold a competition, and choose the best cache design. Then hide it in a public place, uploading its location to geocaching. com for others to find.

Geography

 Most local areas have caches hidden, many in locations that are either important to whoever put them there or represent a key feature of the local area. Arrange a short fieldtrip to explore the local area and search for a number of local caches.

Literacy

 Challenge groups of children to hide a geocache around the school grounds and produce a written description of the location so that other members of the class are able to find the cache after the event. Use small containers for this activity, similar to the old 35mm camera film canisters.

 Hide a variety of caches around the school and place sentence starters inside. These could be linked to the location or topic. Ask individuals or pairs of children to randomly choose one cache location, visit the cache and get their sentence starter. Children then develop a story idea from the text inside.

 Ask the children to record their geocaching adventures in a diary or blog.

Science

 Geocaching relies upon GPS satellites placed around the Earth's surface. Develop children's understanding of space by investigating how these satellites work and what other satellites do in orbit around the Earth.

The following ideas require some preparation and involve children finding caches containing information.

You will need six to ten caches hidden around the school. Record the coordinates of each location on a worksheet so that teams of children can enter them into handheld devices.

History

 After studying or investigating an event, test children on their knowledge of its chronology. Split the event into a number of laminated cards hidden in caches. As children find each cache, they can begin to think about the sequence of sub-events.

Maths

 Set a number of maths challenges and print them onto laminated cards. Children work in teams to visit each cache and solve the mathematical problem inside it.

 As a variation on this theme, create some caches that contain higher-level problems. The children can choose the order in which they approach them. This activity allows the children to demonstrate progression and provides you with useful assessment data.

Music

 Use handheld recording devices to create soundscapes. Hide a number of caches around the school grounds. They should be in places where different sounds can be recorded, for example birdsong, road noise or machinery. Children visit each location and record the sounds there. Back in the classroom, they can turn these into a sound map.

Taking things further

Geocaching is very successful when linked to a whole-school project. For example, one school has hidden caches in and around Box Hill, in Surrey (http://bit.ly/boxhillcache). As the venue for the London 2012 Olympic road race, the caches contain messages to the public about the Olympics and their impact on the environment. They also contain 'travel bugs' – items that travel from cache to cache. They often have an aim, in this case to reach Rio by the next Olympic Games in 2016. The advantage of hiding geocaches in public areas is that a log is kept each time they are found. This is a great way to interact with the local community.

Useful tips and resources

 Approach your ICT coordinator to gain funding for this activity. Some local authorities have class sets of equipment that can be shared.

 Visit www.undertenminutes.com/?p=193 to view a brief video about geocaching.

 Geocaching.com is an excellent resource with many ideas, tips and advice.

 Trails Optional by Jen Deyenberg is an excellent source of Primary geocaching ideas: www.trailsoptional.com/about-me/.

ICT with younger children

The possibilities for covering ICT with younger children depend to a great extent on provision within the early years setting. This may be a computer (a set of) that is constantly available for them to access. If this is the case, it is vital to use sites to share links and make it easy for them to access appropriate content. Small hands often end up clicking where they shouldn't and closing the browser set up by the teacher, so having a page of links for children to access is important.

During the early years, children should be given access to a range of ICT equipment including CD players, as well as being given the chance to use cameras. The majority of the sites below focus on simple skills such as mouse control, dragging and dropping or using the keyboard. These skills are all essential, but be aware that many children will already be comfortable with these when they join the school.

- **Fungooms** – www.fungooms.com Contains short mini-games and activities. One involves clicking on different sources of light in a child's bedroom and another making shapes out of **clouds**.

- **Funbrain** – www.funbrain.com This site is slightly more complicated; it requires a few extra clicks to get started then the children play games and completes activities to move their playing piece around a board.

- **iBoard** – www.iboard.co.uk/ This site continues to grow as more resources are added. It began as a tool for younger children but is now available for Key Stage 2 as well. The activities cover mainly literacy and numeracy but there are others linked to the rest of the curriculum.

- **ICT Games** – www.ictgames.com Boasts a range of maths and literacy games including activities to help with telling the time, counting and spelling.

- **Literactive** – www.literactive.com Has some great resources including a range of storybooks based on traditional tales. These files usually need to be **downloaded** to the computer rather than being played online. The site requires a login.

- **Poisson Rouge** – www.poissonrouge.com This site is a beautiful, crazy, inspirational place for children to explore, offering hours of use. It is particularly suitable for young children as it

A screenshot from Poisson Rouge.

does not include any instructions at all, so children are required to explore and see what happens as they navigate around. The activities range from counting to ten, joining stars to make a picture, creating pop-art images or making music. The castle enables them to build vocabulary in English or French; as children click on the picture the word is displayed. There is a further option to go through the window to try and find the eight missing fruit. There are over 30 activities, some of which have a fruit hidden on them, although many do not.

Google Apps for Education

Google Apps is the name given to a collection of tools from Google that are free for schools. These can all be set up so that the children are given their own accounts, providing them with access to the tools available. The children can also be grouped so that different sets have access to different tools. More and more schools are considering this sort of **cloud** solution as it costs very little compared to **VLE**s. It is also updated regularly and used by millions around the world.

The core tools available through Google Apps are:

 Calendar – Enables you to create calendars for each user or for a group. The calendar could be used to share school events (with children and parents) or to organise a club.

 Docs – An online document creator and editor. Users can create presentations, documents, spreadsheets and forms which can then be shared with other users. These look very similar to other tools, such as Microsoft Office, but enable users to access the files anywhere. The documents can also be embedded into other websites as on the Ideas to Inspire site (www.ideastoinspire.co.uk). As the documents are collaborative, children can create presentations in small groups and then access the document simultaneously. The spreadsheet tool can cope with 50 users at once, making it particularly useful for collecting data from children. For example, they can be given the link to a single document, add their data at the same time to create a set of whole-class results.

 Mail – An email application providing users with 25Gb of storage space, and requiring very little training for children. The application can be set so that children can only email each other rather than anyone outside the school environment. Discuss potential e-safety issues with the children before using email.

Sites – A tool providing children with the opportunity to create websites. Each site can include a range of content such as pictures and links as well as maps, calendars and videos. The sites can be used in numerous ways including creating portfolios of children's work or as an alternative way of presenting work.

Google Apps offers the option to share children's work publically with anyone in the world, to keep something private for the owner or to combine both of these so that the site or document owner chooses who else can view or edit. Users are shown a 'share' window where they can choose who else should have access.

Children can therefore create websites, then opt to keep them between their circle of friends and the teacher. Other features, such as Groups or Picasa, give the administrator control to configure these as necessary.

One of the major benefits of creating Google Apps accounts is that children can also access other services, such as Google Maps, allowing them to create their own story map or Maths Map. They can also be given a YouTube account in a similar manner so check the settings when creating accounts.

When setting up Google Apps, the only cost is to buy a domain name, such as www.stjohnsapps.co.uk. Otherwise, there are no charges for schools. Once a domain has been chosen, the setup wizard takes you through the process of adding users, setting up services and getting started. It is possible to add ten users to the account; this is the maximum number when using the free version, but schools can apply for the education license which will then provide all the accounts they need.

When everything is set up, make sure that you have a landing page, such as www.stjohnsapps.co.uk, so that children can find all the tools in one place. Link this site to the main school website or blog as well.

Using the Google Apps Marketplace, extra features can be added. One of the most useful additional tools for schools is Aviary, which allows users to edit and create audio files.

Useful resources

To get started, visit www.google.com/apps/intl/en/edu/. A guide to setting up Google Apps can be found at http://ianaddison.net/top-5/, showing each step of the creation process.

There is also a range of ideas for using Google Docs on the Ideas to Inspire website (www.ideastoinspire. com).

CHAPTER 13 HOW TO ...

Introduction

This chapter demonstrates how to complete a selection of key ICT tasks to enhance teaching and learning in the classroom, including **embedding** content within websites or **blogs**, shortening website addresses and resizing photos. These tasks have all been referred to throughout the book, and this chapter aims to promote an understanding of how they work and how they can be achieved. It also provides an explanation as to why these are useful skills to have.

For how-to guides for other **software**, visit Under Ten Minutes (www.undertenminutes.com).

Shortening website addresses

Why?

This is particularly useful with website addresses that are too long or complicated to share easily. If the link is put on another website, it can be clicked and there is no need to shorten the address. However, if it is displayed somewhere (for example in a book such as this) or is added to paper-based media such as a school newsletter or leaflet, a shorter **URL** is helpful.

TOP TIP

People often enter an address into a search engine, such as Google, rather than directly into the address bar. Searching in this way for short URLs will probably not work in most cases.

How?

Using sites such as TinyURL (www.tiny.cc) or Bit.ly (www.bit.ly), simply paste in the long address and the site will convert it into a shortened version. However, this is usually in the form of random letters and numbers such as http://tiny.cc/iov3cw, in all likelihood more complicated than the original address. There is an alternative to this, known as a custom URL. This can be

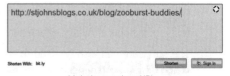
bit.ly shortens long URLs.

any selection of letters, words or numbers – providing it is available. Many links in this book have been created in this way, including the tour of St John's school on Animoto (http://bit.ly/stjohnstour).

To create a custom URL in Bit.ly, users need to sign up for a free account. The benefit of signing up is that all links are subsequently made available in a central location and statistics provided to show how often the site has been clicked on.

Resizing photographs

Why?

Schools are taking and storing hundreds (if not thousands) of photographs each year, and therefore need to monitor the size of these photographs so they do not take up too much space on the computer. This takes up space on the school server as new photos are added each year but more importantly is their use **online**. Larger pictures take longer to **upload**, longer to **download** and use more space. Using up space has two possible disadvantages: if the tool you are using is free, it may have limited space available; if you pay for webspace you may soon need to buy more as photo use increases.

As cameras have produced pictures with more and more **megapixels** (MP), the size of photographs has increased. Always consider how and when these pictures are used – a chart at http://bit.ly/ howmanypixels shows that 8MP can produce an impressive A4 printout. But how often in school are pictures of this size used? If the answer is never, then shrinking them to A5 will make more sense.

How?

The first step is to visit the camera. Check the resolution in the settings and take it down from the highest setting to around 4–6MP (see page 10). Future images will be much smaller but still of sufficient quality for school use. If a need for a higher-quality image arises, readjust the settings as necessary.

If you are resizing just one image, tools such as Pic Resize (www.picresize.com/) do this within seconds. In most cases, however, you may need to resize a whole folder of images – this is where **software** will need to be downloaded. There are many possibilities available, and a popular one in schools is Microsoft Picture Manager. This comes as part of Microsoft Office and a guide to using it to resize photos is available at http://bit.ly/resizepics. A video is also available on Under Ten Minutes (www. undertenminutes.com).

The software can also be used to crop images and, as it is usually installed on every computer in the school, there is no need for additional tools to be downloaded.

Embedding content

Embeddable content is content that can be taken from one website and put onto another. This could include a photo slideshow, a word search or a video. Some sites provide embed codes written in **HTML** that allow content to be included in a blog or website elsewhere. Within the school context, the main places to embed content are on a class blog, website or **VLE**.

Why?

Embedding content makes navigation much easier than expecting the viewer to click on a link to find the content elsewhere. It also makes the blog, for example, more attractive, as the content appears on the page rather than elsewhere via a clickable link.

How?

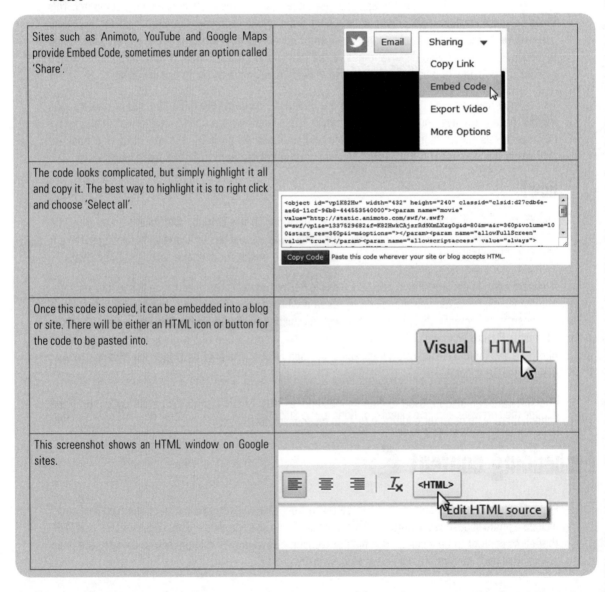

Sites such as Animoto, YouTube and Google Maps provide Embed Code, sometimes under an option called 'Share'.	
The code looks complicated, but simply highlight it all and copy it. The best way to highlight it is to right click and choose 'Select all'.	
Once this code is copied, it can be embedded into a blog or site. There will be either an HTML icon or button for the code to be pasted into.	
This screenshot shows an HTML window on Google sites.	

Taking screenshots

It is possible to take a snapshot of the computer screen so that the picture can be used elsewhere. This is particularly useful when creating how-to guides or for demonstrating to the children how to achieve a particular goal.

Why?

When presenting a new piece of software, it is useful to highlight a particular option or element using a screenshot. Screenshots are also useful for the **avatar** creation tools that do not provide an option to save the image to the computer.

How?

In most cases, the most straightforward option is to press the Print Screen button, which will then copy the entire screen. Then open a paint package, such as Paint, and paste the image onto the canvas. This can then be cropped as required.

One option for Windows 7 users is to use the Snipping tool. This is a built-in tool that will cut a small section of the screen to then either paste it elsewhere or save it as a picture.

The 'snipped' section can be a rectangular shape or there is also an option to draw a free-form image.

The Snipping tool being used to take a screenshot in Animoto.

If the Snipping tool is not available, the Print-Screen tool from Gadwin is a useful alternative (www.gadwin.com/download/). Once installed, this can be set up so that when the Print-Screen key is pressed, it loads the software and gives similar options to the Snipping tool, allowing small portions of the screen to be captured and used elsewhere.

CHAPTER 14 USEFUL LINKS

- **ICT Magic** – http://ictmagic.wikispaces.com This award-winning site is an impressive collection of resources and ideas that grows daily. There are websites for every curriculum subject and many other areas too, such as cookery, classroom management and languages.

- **ICT Planning** – www.ictplanning.co.uk An ICT planning site where the curriculum has been divided into a range of topics so that it works as an ICT menu. The objectives and lessons are not organised by year group or age, but rather by ability. There is a range of lesson plans for a number of the tools used within this book. For each tool on the site there are links to how-to guides, lesson plans and possible ways of using it within the curriculum.

- **Interesting Ways to …** – http://edte.ch/blog/interesting-ways/ An idea started by Tom Barrett, the site includes a range of shared presentations created using Google Docs, covering a variety of ideas of software tools. Each page of a presentation contains a new idea; these ideas have been collected online from people who have found resources via Twitter or Tom's blog.

- **PGCE Guide** – www.pgceguide.com/ and **NQT Guide** – http://nqtguide.co.uk/ These online guides have been organised by Tim Handley, a newly qualified teacher (NQT) from Norfolk. They present a collection of ideas and articles from trainee teachers, NQTs and experienced teachers.

- **Teaching Websites** – www.teachingwebsites.co.uk/ These incredibly useful sites, created by Mark Warner, are useful for a range of different purposes, including showcasing handy apps to download for use in the classroom or sharing lesson plans and teaching ideas.

- **Under Ten Minutes** – www.undertenminutes.com The aim of this site is to show how to use a piece of software in less than ten minutes. Where possible, videos are accompanied by useful blog posts, documentation, links and other useful resources. The videos tend to be hosted on YouTube. Some videos have also been created by children.

GLOSSARY

Glossary

Application Often abbreviated to 'app'. An application is a program that enables you to perform a range of useful tasks. These are often found on mobile devices but can also be included in a browser, for example Chrome has an app-store.

Avatar The name given to an online character that can be used to represent a physical person. This could be used instead of a 'real' photograph when displaying a profile picture.

Blog This is a website where users, or groups of users, post updates on a regular basis. Each time an update is posted, the others are pushed further down the screen. This works well for news items and in schools for sharing learning.

Browser This is a piece of **software** used for retrieving and presenting resources and websites from the **internet**. Internet Explorer is the browser that is included with Windows while Safari is used on iPods and Mac computers. Other browsers include Firefox and Google Chrome.

Clipart Pre-made illustrations that can be used to enhance or decorate a piece of work. These are often included in a library for users to add to their document or page.

Cloud This is the term for tools and applications that are available **online**. It means that they can be accessed from a computer anywhere in the world rather than just on one computer. Email has been cloud-based for many years but now more and more **software** is available online. Google **Apps** and Microsoft Office365 are tools where documents and files can be stored in the cloud too.

Creative Commmons License This is a set of guidelines and licenses for sharing content on the web. More information can be found.

Download To get a file or a substantial piece of information from the internet and transfer it to your computer or mobile device.

Embedding This is the term for taking content from one place and putting it in another. This could involve taking a video from YouTube and embedding it on the school website. The video is technically still on YouTube, but is visible on the school site and can be played as normal.

Hardware The name given to physical devices that connect to a computer such as a monitor, a mouse or a scanner. The word peripheral can also be used for some of these types of equipment.

HTML (Hyper-Text Markup Language) This describes the set of codes and elements that many websites are written in. It is the basic building block for the **internet.**

Internet A global network of devices connected together via phone lines and data cables.

Login To identify yourself to the system, so that you can access the file or information. The most common way is to type in a **username** and **password** that the system will recognise as yours.

Megapixel This is the name given to a million pixels and is used to describe the resolution of a digital camera, e.g. a 5-Megapixel camera.

Menu A list of options or commands in a computer program. Often found along the toolbar at the top of the screen.

MP3 An acronym for MPEG layer 3. This is the standard format for compressing sounds into a very small file, up to 12 times smaller. There is normally little or no loss of sound quality.

Network A system of connected computers or devices that could also include printers. This is often controlled by a server.

Offline The term given when not connected to the **internet** or a **network**.

Online The term given when connected to the **internet** or a **network**.

Password A word, phrase or combination of letters that is used to gain access to secure sites.

PDF (Portable Document Format) A file format developed by Adobe, which is nearly always read-only, making it useful for distributing to people as it cannot be changed by them. Acrobat Reader is a free program that can be downloaded from www.getadobe.com/uk/reader and allows you to open and read PDF files.

Pixel This is the name given to a small area of the screen that illuminates to form a picture or display.

Plugin This is a set of **software** components that adds specific capabilities to a larger software application such as a web **browser**.

SD (Secure Digital) card This is the most common form of memory card used in digital cameras and it stores information and images.

Skype A piece of software that gives users the opportunity to make voice calls via the **internet**, usually for free. Skype can also be used to call landline and mobile numbers but this will be charged for.

Software The name given to programs used by a computer.

Tags Tags are keywords used for describing a picture or resource, and are used when you are searching the **internet**. Resources can have multiple tags, for example one picture could be tagged with 'elephant', 'Africa' and 'endangered'. Entering any of these search terms will show the picture.

Upload To transfer a data file from your personal computer or mobile device to a server or the **internet**.

URL (Uniform Resource Locator) This is the address of a webpage, for example www.google.co.uk.

USB (Universal Serial Bus) A type of connector that links devices together, such as keyboards, printers, digital cameras, etc.

VLE (Virtual Learning Environment) Also known as a Learning Platform, this is usually a product containing many different elements for learning, teaching and management in one place. It could be a paid-for product or one designed by the school. The VLE may include features for messaging other children, sharing learning, setting homework, accessing resources and links and for calendars. These VLEs are often referred to as 'walled gardens' as the content is locked to users of a particular place, for example the school only.

Web 2.0 This is a term to describe the way in which people interact with the internet. When the **internet** began, most people were consumers, viewing and accessing resources. With Web 2.0 sites people are now producers of content as well as consumers, for example creators of **blogs**, videos, Facebook comments or websites.

Webcam A video camera that connects to the computer to transfer a video image. It can also be used to record video or still images or for animating movies.

Weblink The address of a website.

Widget A small piece of **software** that can be used to add additional features or information to a webpage. For example, this could be a map of visitors to your **blog**. The terms **plugins** and widgets are often interchangeable.